ASIAN COOKING

STIR-FRIES, BOWLS, NOODLES, SNACKS, DRINKS AND MORE

pil

Publications International, Ltd.

Pictured on the front cover: Chicken Ramen Noodle Bowls (page 106).

Pictured on the back cover (counterclockwise from top left): Chinese Peppercorn Beef (page 156), Lobster Pot Stickers (page 22), Chickpea Tikka Masala (page 178) and Orange-Ginger Ramen Slaw (page 42).

ISBN: 978-1-64030-447-5

Manufactured in China.

8 7 6 5 4 3 2 1

TABLE OF CONTENTS

SNACKS & DRINKS 4

SALADS, SOUPS & VEGETABLES 38

FROM THE WOK 68

BOWLS 98

NOODLES 110

MEAT, CHICKEN & SEAFOOD 126

INDIAN INSPIRED 164

INDEX 188

SNACKS & DRINKS

MINI EGG ROLLS
MAKES 28 EGG ROLLS

8   ounces ground pork

3   cloves garlic, minced

1   teaspoon minced fresh
    ginger or ginger paste

¼   teaspoon red pepper
    flakes

6   cups (12 ounces)
    shredded coleslaw mix

¼   cup soy sauce

1   tablespoon cornstarch

1   tablespoon rice vinegar

½   cup chopped green
    onions

28 wonton wrappers

    Peanut or canola oil for
    frying

    Sweet and sour sauce and
    chinese hot mustard

1 Combine pork, garlic, ginger and red pepper flakes in large nonstick skillet; cook and stir over medium heat about 4 minutes or until pork is cooked through, stirring to break up meat. Add coleslaw mix; cover and cook 2 minutes. Uncover and cook 2 minutes or until coleslaw mix just begins to wilt.

2 Whisk soy sauce into cornstarch in small bowl until smooth and well blended; stir into pork mixture. Add vinegar; cook 2 to 3 minutes or until sauce is thickened. Remove from heat; stir in green onions.

3 Working with one at a time, place wonton wrapper on work surface with point facing you. Spoon level tablespoon of pork mixture across and just below center of wrapper. Fold bottom point of wrapper up over filling; fold side points over filling, forming envelope shape. Moisten inside edges of top point with water and roll up toward top point, pressing firmly to seal. Repeat with remaining wrappers and filling.

4 Heat ¼ inch of oil in large deep skillet to 375°F. Fry egg rolls in small batches 2 minutes per side or until golden brown. Remove with slotted spoon and drain on paper towels. Serve immediately with sweet and sour sauce and mustard for dipping.

SWEET AND SPICY CHICKEN WINGS

MAKES 4 TO 6 SERVINGS

DIP

- ½ cup ranch dressing
- 2 tablespoons buttermilk
- 1 teaspoon prepared horseradish
- ½ teaspoon wasabi

SAUCE

- ¾ cup water
- 1 tablespoon cornstarch
- ¼ cup packed dark brown sugar
- ¼ cup soy sauce
- 3 tablespoons lime juice
- 2 tablespoons minced fresh ginger
- 1 teaspoon minced garlic
- ¼ teaspoon red pepper flakes

CHICKEN

- 2 pounds boneless skinless chicken breasts
- 1 cup all-purpose flour
- ¼ cup cornstarch
- 2 teaspoons salt
- ¼ teaspoon black pepper
- ¼ teaspoon ground red pepper
- ¼ teaspoon paprika
- 2 eggs
- ½ cup milk
- Vegetable oil for frying

1 For dip, combine ranch dressing, buttermilk, horseradish and wasabi in small bowl; mix well. Refrigerate until ready to use.

2 For sauce, whisk water and 1 tablespoon cornstarch in medium saucepan until smooth. Add brown sugar, soy sauce, lime juice, ginger, garlic and red pepper flakes; whisk until well blended. Bring to a boil over high heat. Reduce heat to low; simmer 10 minutes or until thickened, stirring occasionally. Transfer to large bowl; set aside to cool.

3 Cut chicken into large pieces (about 2×1 inches). Combine flour, ¼ cup cornstarch, salt, black pepper, ground red pepper and paprika in large bowl. Whisk eggs and milk in shallow bowl. Coat chicken with flour mixture. Dip in egg mixture, letting excess drip back into bowl. Coat again with flour mixture; place on baking sheet.

4 Heat 3 inches of oil in large saucepan over medium-high heat to 375°F; adjust heat to maintain temperature. Cook chicken in batches 3 minutes or until golden brown and cooked through, turning once. Drain on paper towel-lined plate. Add chicken to sauce and stir to coat. Remove to serving plate with slotted spoon. Serve with dip.

ASIAN LETTUCE WRAPS

MAKES ABOUT 6 SERVINGS

2 teaspoons canola oil

1½ pounds boneless skinless chicken breasts or pork shoulder, chopped into ¼-inch pieces

2 leeks, white and green parts, coarsely chopped

1 cup shiitake mushrooms, stemmed and chopped

1 stalk celery, cut into ¼-inch pieces

1 tablespoon oyster sauce

1 tablespoon soy sauce

1 teaspoon dark sesame oil

¼ teaspoon ground black pepper

2 tablespoons water

1 bag (8 ounces) coleslaw or broccoli slaw mix

½ red bell pepper, cut into thin strips

8 ounces large raw shrimp, peeled, deveined and cut into ¼-inch pieces

3 tablespoons salted dry-roasted peanuts, coarsely chopped

Hoisin sauce

12 to 15 leaves crisp romaine lettuce, white rib removed and patted dry

Fresh chives (optional)

SLOW COOKER DIRECTIONS

1 Heat oil in large skillet over medium-high heat. Add chicken; cook and stir until browned on all sides. Transfer to slow cooker. Stir in leeks, mushrooms, celery, oyster sauce, soy sauce, sesame oil, black pepper and water. Place bell pepper and coleslaw mix in single layer on top of chicken.

2 Cover; cook on LOW 4 to 5 hours or on HIGH 2 to 2½ hours or until chicken is cooked through. Stir in shrimp during last 20 minutes of cooking. When shrimp are pink and opaque, transfer mixture to large bowl. Add chopped peanuts; mix well.

3 To serve, spread about 1 teaspoon hoisin sauce on lettuce leaf. Add 1 to 2 tablespoons meat mixture and tightly roll up; secure by tying chives around rolled leaves, if desired. Repeat with remaining ingredients.

NOTE: Be sure to rinse leeks thoroughly under cold water to remove dirt and debris from between layers.

WASABI ROASTED EDAMAME

MAKES 4 TO 6 SERVINGS

2 teaspoons vegetable oil

2 teaspoons honey

¼ teaspoon wasabi powder

1 package (10 ounces) shelled edamame, thawed if frozen

Kosher salt (optional)

1 Preheat oven to 375°F.

2 Combine oil, honey and wasabi powder in large bowl; mix well. Add edamame; toss to coat. Spread on baking sheet in single layer.

3 Bake 12 to 15 minutes or until golden brown, stirring once. Immediately remove from baking sheet to large bowl; sprinkle generously with salt, if desired. Cool completely before serving. Store leftovers in airtight container.

SATAY BEEF

MAKES 4 SERVINGS

1 pound beef tenderloin steaks

5 tablespoons water, divided

3½ teaspoons soy sauce, divided

2 teaspoons dark sesame oil

1 teaspoon cornstarch

2 tablespoons vegetable oil

1 medium yellow onion, coarsely chopped

1 clove garlic, minced

1 tablespoon dry sherry

1 tablespoon satay sauce

1 teaspoon curry powder

½ teaspoon sugar

1 Cut beef crosswise into thin slices; flatten each slice by pressing with fingers. Place in medium bowl.

2 Stir 3 tablespoons water, 1½ teaspoons soy sauce and sesame oil into cornstarch in small bowl. Add to beef; stir to coat well. Let stand 20 minutes.

3 Heat vegetable oil in wok or large skillet over high heat. Add half of beef in single layer. Cook 2 to 3 minutes per side or just until lightly browned. Remove from wok; set aside. Repeat with remaining beef.

4 Add onion and garlic to wok; stir-fry about 3 minutes or until tender.

5 Combine remaining 2 tablespoons water, 2 teaspoons soy sauce, sherry, satay sauce, curry powder and sugar in small bowl. Add to wok; bring to a boil. Cook and stir until liquid boils. Return beef to wok; cook and stir until heated through.

SPICED ORANGE CHICKEN KABOB APPETIZERS

MAKES 12 SERVINGS

8 boneless skinless chicken breasts

1 red or green bell pepper

24 small white mushrooms

½ cup orange juice

2 tablespoons soy sauce

1 tablespoon vegetable oil

1½ teaspoons onion powder

½ teaspoon Chinese five-spice powder

1 Cut chicken and bell pepper into 24 (¾-inch) cubes. Place chicken, bell pepper and mushrooms in large resealable food storage bag.

2 Combine orange juice, soy sauce, oil, onion powder and five-spice powder in small bowl. Pour over chicken and vegetables. Seal bag; turn to coat. Marinate in refrigerator 4 to 24 hours, turning occasionally.

3 Soak 24 small wooden skewers or toothpicks in water 20 minutes. Meanwhile, preheat broiler. Coat broiler pan with nonstick cooking spray.

4 Drain chicken mixture, reserving marinade. Thread 1 piece of chicken, 1 piece of bell pepper and 1 mushroom onto each skewer. Place on prepared pan. Brush with marinade; discard remaining marinade. Broil 4 inches from heat 5 to 6 minutes or until chicken is no longer pink in center. Serve immediately.

GINGER CHICKEN POT STICKERS

MAKES 24 POT STICKERS

3 cups finely shredded cabbage

4 green onions, finely chopped

1 egg white, lightly beaten

1 tablespoon soy sauce

1 tablespoon minced fresh ginger

¼ teaspoon plus ⅛ teaspoon red pepper flakes, divided

4 ounces ground chicken breast, cooked and drained

24 wonton wrappers, at room temperature

½ cup water

1 tablespoon cornstarch

1 tablespoon oyster sauce

2 teaspoons grated lemon peel

½ teaspoon honey

1 tablespoon peanut oil

1 Steam cabbage in steamer basket over boiling water 5 minutes; cool to room temperature.

2 Meanwhile, combine green onions, egg white, soy sauce, ginger and ¼ teaspoon red pepper flakes in large bowl; mix well. Stir in chicken. Squeeze out excess moisture from cabbage; stir into bowl.

3 Working with one at a time, place wonton wrapper on clean work surface. Brush edges of wrapper with water. Place 1 tablespoon filling in center of wrapper; pinch edges together to seal. Place on baking sheet dusted with cornstarch. Repeat with remaining wrappers and filling. Refrigerate 1 hour or until cold.

4 Meanwhile, whisk ½ cup water, cornstarch, oyster sauce, lemon peel, honey and remaining ⅛ teaspoon red pepper flakes in small bowl until well blended.

5 Heat oil in large nonstick skillet over high heat. Place pot stickers in skillet flat sides down; cook until bottoms are golden brown. Pour sauce over top; cover and cook 3 minutes. Uncover and cook until all liquid is absorbed. Serve immediately.

CHINESE CRAB CAKES

MAKES 4 SERVINGS

1 pound fresh* or canned pasteurized lump crabmeat

½ cup plus ⅓ cup panko bread crumbs, divided

2 eggs

2 green onions, finely chopped

1 tablespoon dark sesame oil

1 tablespoon grated fresh ginger

1 tablespoon Chinese hot mustard

2 tablespoons peanut or canola oil, divided

½ cup sweet and sour sauce

Choose special grade crabmeat for this recipe. It is less expensive and already flaked but just as flavorful as backfin, lump or claw meat. Look for it in the refrigerated seafood section of the supermarket. Shelf-stable canned crabmeat can be substituted.

1 Combine crabmeat, ½ cup panko, eggs, green onions, sesame oil, ginger and mustard in large bowl; mix well.

2 Shape level ⅓ cupfuls of mixture into 8 patties about ½ inch thick. (At this point patties may be covered and chilled up to 2 hours.)

3 Place remaining ⅓ cup panko in shallow dish; dip each crab cake lightly in panko to coat. Heat 1 tablespoon peanut oil in large nonstick skillet over medium heat. Add 4 crab cakes; cook 3 to 4 minutes per side or until golden brown and heated through. (Crab cakes will be soft, so turn them carefully.) Keep warm. Repeat with remaining 1 tablespoon oil and 4 crab cakes. Serve with sweet and sour sauce.

SWEET-HOT ORANGE CHICKEN DRUMETTES

MAKES ABOUT 5 SERVINGS

¼ cup plus 3 tablespoons orange juice, divided

4 tablespoons orange marmalade or apricot jam, divided

3 tablespoons hoisin sauce

1 teaspoon grated fresh ginger

10 chicken drumettes (about 1¼ pounds)

3 tablespoons chili garlic sauce

¼ teaspoon salt

¼ teaspoon red pepper flakes

⅛ teaspoon Chinese five-spice powder (optional)

⅛ teaspoon black pepper

Sesame seeds (optional)

1 Preheat oven to 400°F. Line baking sheet with heavy-duty foil; generously spray foil with nonstick cooking spray.

2 Combine ¼ cup orange juice, 2 tablespoons orange marmalade, hoisin sauce and ginger in medium microwavable bowl. Microwave on HIGH 1 minute or until marmalade melts; stir until well blended.

3 Dip drumettes, one at a time, in orange juice mixture; place on prepared baking sheet. Bake 15 minutes; turn and bake 5 to 10 minutes or until drumettes are golden brown and cooked through.

4 Meanwhile for dipping sauce, combine remaining 3 tablespoons orange juice, 2 tablespoons orange marmalade, chili garlic sauce, salt, red pepper flakes, five-spice powder, if desired, and black pepper in small microwavable bowl. Microwave on HIGH 1 minute or until marmalade melts; stir until well blended.

5 Sprinkle sesame seeds over chicken; serve with dipping sauce.

LOBSTER POT STICKERS

MAKES ABOUT 26 POT STICKERS

4 dried black Chinese mushrooms

¼ cup plus 2 teaspoons soy sauce, divided

3 teaspoons dark sesame oil, divided

1 tablespoon rice vinegar

8 ounces lobster-flavored surimi, finely chopped

2 cups chopped napa or green cabbage

¼ cup chopped green onions

1 tablespoon minced fresh ginger

26 wonton wrappers

2 tablespoons vegetable oil, divided

1 cup chicken broth, divided

1 Place mushrooms in large bowl; cover with hot water. Soak 30 minutes or until soft.

2 Meanwhile for sauce, whisk ¼ cup soy sauce, 1 teaspoon sesame oil and rice vinegar in small bowl until well blended; set aside.

3 Drain mushrooms; discard water. Cut off and discard stems. Chop caps; return to bowl. Add surimi, cabbage, green onions, ginger, remaining 2 teaspoons sesame oil and 2 teaspoons soy sauce; gently toss to combine.

4 Working with a few at a time, arrange wonton wrappers on clean work surface. Cut ½-inch triangle off all corners of wrappers to make rounded shapes. Place about 2 teaspoons surimi mixture in center of each wrapper. Lightly moisten edges with water; fold in half. Pinch edges together to seal. Keep finished pot stickers covered with plastic wrap while filling remaining wrappers.

5 Heat 1 tablespoon vegetable oil in large nonstick skillet over medium heat. Add half of pot stickers; cook 5 to 6 minutes or until bottoms are golden brown, turning once.

6 Pour ½ cup broth into skillet; reduce heat to low. Cover and simmer 10 minutes or until all liquid is absorbed. Repeat with remaining vegetable oil, pot stickers and broth. Serve immediately with sauce for dipping.

TIP: Pot stickers may be cooked immediately or covered and refrigerated up to 4 hours or frozen up to 3 months. To freeze, place pot stickers on cookie sheet or shallow pan; freeze 30 minutes to firm slightly. Transfer to freezer food storage bag. Frozen pot stickers do not need to be thawed before cooking.

SPICY CRISPY SHRIMP

MAKES 4 SERVINGS

SAUCE

½ cup mayonnaise

4 teaspoons Thai chili sauce

1 teaspoon honey

½ teaspoon rice vinegar

SHRIMP

¾ cup buttermilk

1 egg

¾ cup all-purpose flour

½ cup panko bread crumbs

1 teaspoon salt

½ teaspoon ground sage

½ teaspoon black pepper

¼ teaspoon onion powder

¼ teaspoon garlic powder

¼ teaspoon dried basil

16 to 20 large raw shrimp, peeled, deveined and patted dry

Vegetable oil for frying

2 green onions, thinly sliced (optional)

1 For sauce, combine mayonnaise, chili sauce, honey and vinegar in large bowl; mix well. Cover and refrigerate until ready to serve.

2 Whisk buttermilk and egg in medium bowl until well blended. Combine flour, panko, salt, sage, pepper, onion powder, garlic powder and basil in separate medium bowl; mix well. Dip each shrimp in buttermilk mixture, then in flour mixture, turning to coat completely. Place breaded shrimp on large plate; refrigerate until oil is hot.

3 Heat 2 inches of oil in large saucepan over medium-high heat to 350°F; adjust heat to maintain temperature. Cook shrimp, 4 to 6 at a time, 2 to 3 minutes or until golden brown, turning halfway through cooking time. Drain on paper towel-lined plate.

4 Add shrimp to sauce; toss gently to coat. Garnish with green onions.

SPICY CHICKEN BUNDLES

MAKES 12 APPETIZERS

1 pound ground chicken or turkey

2 teaspoons minced fresh ginger

2 cloves garlic, minced

¼ teaspoon red pepper flakes

3 tablespoons soy sauce

1 tablespoon cornstarch

1 tablespoon peanut or vegetable oil

⅓ cup finely chopped water chestnuts

⅓ cup thinly sliced green onions

¼ cup chopped peanuts

12 large lettuce leaves, such as romaine or Bibb

Fresh chives (optional)

Chinese hot mustard (optional)

1 Combine chicken, ginger, garlic and red pepper flakes in medium bowl. Stir soy sauce into cornstarch in small bowl until smooth.

2 Heat oil in wok or large skillet over medium-high heat. Add chicken mixture; cook and stir 2 to 3 minutes until chicken is cooked through.

3 Stir soy sauce mixture; add to wok. Stir-fry 30 seconds or until sauce boils and thickens. Add water chestnuts, green onions and peanuts; heat through.

4 Divide filling evenly among lettuce leaves; roll up. Secure with toothpicks or tie with fresh chives. Serve warm or at room temperature. Serve with hot mustard, if desired.

MINI MARINATED BEEF SKEWERS

MAKES 18 SKEWERS

1 boneless beef top round
  steak (about 1 pound)

2 tablespoons soy sauce

1 tablespoon dry sherry

1 teaspoon dark sesame oil

2 cloves garlic, minced

1 Cut beef crosswise into 18 (⅛-inch-thick) slices. Place in large resealable food storage bag. Combine soy sauce, sherry, oil and garlic in small cup; pour over beef. Seal bag; turn to coat. Marinate in refrigerator at least 30 minutes or up to 2 hours.

2 Meanwhile, soak 18 (6-inch) wooden skewers in water 20 minutes.

3 Preheat broiler. Drain beef; discard marinade. Weave beef accordion-style onto skewers. Place on rack of broiler pan.

4 Broil 4 to 5 inches from heat 2 minutes. Turn skewers over; broil 2 minutes more or until beef is barely pink. Serve warm.

SCALLION PANCAKES

MAKES 32 WEDGES

2 cups all-purpose flour

1 teaspoon sugar

⅔ cup boiling water

¼ to ½ cup cold water

2 teaspoons dark sesame oil

½ cup finely chopped green onion tops

1 teaspoon coarse salt

½ to ¾ cup vegetable oil

1 Combine flour and sugar in large bowl. Stir in boiling water and mix with chopsticks or fork just until water is absorbed and mixture forms large clumps. Gradually stir in enough cold water until dough forms a ball and is no longer sticky.

2 Place dough on lightly floured surface; flatten slightly. Knead 5 minutes or until dough is smooth and elastic. Wrap with plastic wrap; let stand 1 hour.

3 Unwrap dough and knead briefly on lightly floured surface; divide dough into four pieces. Roll one piece into 6- to 7-inch circle, keeping remaining pieces wrapped in plastic wrap to prevent drying out. Brush dough with ½ teaspoon sesame oil; sprinkle evenly with 2 tablespoons green onions and ¼ teaspoon salt. Roll up into tight cylinder.

4 Coil cylinder into a spiral and pinch end under into dough. Repeat with remaining dough pieces, sesame oil, green onions and salt. Cover with plastic wrap and let stand 15 minutes.

5 Roll each coiled piece of dough into 6- to 7-inch round on lightly floured surface with floured rolling pin.

6 Heat ½ cup vegetable oil in wok or large skillet over medium-high heat to 375°F. Adjust heat to maintain temperature. Carefully place one pancake into hot oil. Fry 2 to 3 minutes per side or until golden. While pancake is frying, press center lightly with metal spatula to ensure even cooking. Remove to paper towels to drain. Repeat with remaining pancakes, adding additional oil if necessary.

7 Cut each pancake into 8 wedges. Serve immediately.

ALMOND MILK TEA WITH TAPIOCA

MAKES 2 (10-OUNCE) SERVINGS

3½ cups water

2 black tea bags

4 teaspoons sugar

¼ teaspoon almond extract

1 tablespoon quick-cooking tapioca

4 tablespoons whole milk

Ice cubes

1 Bring water to a boil in medium saucepan over medium-high heat.

2 Pour 2 cups boiling water over tea bags in teapot or 2-cup heatproof measuring cup. Steep tea 4 minutes or until very dark. Remove and discard tea bags. Stir in sugar and almond extract; cool to room temperature.

3 Meanwhile, return remaining water to a boil. Add tapioca; boil 3 to 4 minutes or until tapioca is translucent and cooked through. Drain tapioca in fine-mesh strainer; rinse under cold water until cool.

4 Divide tapioca between 2 tall glasses; pour 2 tablespoons milk into each glass. Fill each glass three-fourths full with ice. Divide tea between glasses; stir to combine. Serve immediately.

MELON BUBBLE TEA

MAKES 5 SERVINGS

6 cups water

2 green tea bags

⅓ cup sugar

½ cup black or pastel
   tapioca pearls*

4 cups cubed melon
   (cantaloupe, honeydew
   or watermelon)

2 cups orange juice

½ cup canned coconut milk

4 cups ice cubes

*Large specialty tapioca pearls
specifically designed for bubble
teas are available in Asian markets
and gourmet food stores.*

1 Bring water to a boil in medium saucepan over high heat. Place tea bags in 2-cup heatproof liquid measuring cup. Pour 2 cups boiling water over tea bags. Let steep 5 minutes. Remove and discard tea bags. Stir in sugar. Cool completely.

2 Meanwhile, return remaining water to a boil; add tapioca pearls. Stir gently, allowing pearls float to top. Reduce heat to low; simmer, uncovered, 25 minutes.

3 Remove from heat; let stand 25 minutes or until pearls are chewy and translucent. Drain and rinse under cold water. Combine pearls and tea in glass pitcher. Refrigerate until cold.

4 Combine melon, orange juice, coconut milk and ice in blender or food processor; process until smooth.

5 Place ¼ cup tapioca mixture in bottom of five glasses. Pour in melon mixture. Serve immediately.

GREEN TEA LYCHEE FRAPPÉ

MAKES 2 (10-OUNCE) SERVINGS

1 can (15 ounces) lychees in syrup,* undrained

2 cups water

2 slices peeled fresh ginger (2×¼ inches)

3 green tea bags

Fresh orange slices and cherries (optional)

Canned lychees are available in either the canned fruit or ethnic foods section of most large supermarkets.

1 Drain lychees, reserving syrup. Place lychees in single layer in medium resealable food storage bag; freeze 1 hour or until firm. Cover syrup and refrigerate.

2 Bring water and ginger to a boil in small saucepan over medium-high heat. Pour over tea bags in teapot or 2-cup heatproof measuring cup; steep 3 minutes. Discard ginger and tea bags. Cover tea; refrigerate until cool.

3 Combine frozen lychees, chilled green tea and ½ cup reserved syrup in blender or food processor; blend 20 seconds or until smooth.

4 Pour into two glasses. Garnish with orange slices and cherries. Serve immediately.

NOTE: Lychees are subtropical fruit grown in China, Mexico and the United States. They are small oval fruit with rough, bright red hulls, a single seed and sweet, juicy flesh. Fresh lychees are available in Asian markets in the United States in early summer.

SALADS, SOUPS & VEGETABLES

BUTTERNUT SQUASH IN COCONUT MILK

MAKES 4 TO 6 SERVINGS

2 teaspoons vegetable oil

½ small onion, finely chopped

2 cloves garlic, minced

1 cup canned coconut milk

¼ cup packed brown sugar

1 tablespoon fish sauce or soy sauce

⅛ to ¼ teaspoon red pepper flakes

1 butternut squash (about 2 pounds), peeled and cut into large cubes

⅓ cup flaked coconut

1 tablespoon chopped fresh cilantro

1 Heat oil in large saucepan over medium-high heat. Add onion and garlic; cook and stir 3 minutes or until tender. Add coconut milk, brown sugar, fish sauce and red pepper flakes; stir until sugar is dissolved.

2 Bring mixture to a boil; add squash. Reduce heat to medium; cover and simmer 30 minutes or until squash is tender.

3 Meanwhile, toast coconut in medium dry skillet over medium-low heat until golden, stirring frequently.

4 Transfer squash to serving bowl with slotted spoon. Increase heat to high; boil remaining liquid until thick, stirring constantly. Pour liquid over squash in bowl. Sprinkle with toasted coconut and chopped cilantro.

HOT AND SOUR SOUP

MAKES 4 TO 5 SERVINGS

2 cans (about 14 ounces each) chicken broth

1 can (4 ounces) sliced mushrooms

2 tablespoons rice vinegar or white wine vinegar

¼ to ½ teaspoon hot pepper sauce

2 tablespoons soy sauce

2 tablespoons cornstarch

1 egg, lightly beaten

2 green onions, chopped

1 Combine broth, mushrooms, vinegar and ¼ teaspoon hot pepper sauce in medium saucepan. Bring to a boil over high heat.

2 Stir soy sauce into cornstarch in small bowl until smooth. Stir into soup. Reduce heat to medium-high; cook and stir until slightly thickened.

3 Gradually pour in egg, stirring in one direction 1 minute or until egg is cooked. Remove from heat; stir in green onions. Season to taste with additional hot pepper sauce.

TIP: For a heartier soup, add shredded cooked chicken to the broth before thickening it.

ORANGE-GINGER RAMEN SLAW

MAKES 6 TO 8 SERVINGS

1 package (3 ounces) ramen noodles, any flavor, coarsely crumbled*

1 tablespoon sesame seeds

6 cups finely shredded green cabbage

2 cups shredded carrots

½ cup diced red onion

½ cup raisins

¾ cup orange marmalade, microwaved for 30 seconds

¼ cup cider vinegar

¼ cup canola oil

3 tablespoons grated fresh ginger

1 tablespoon soy sauce

1 teaspoon grated orange peel (optional)

1 teaspoon hot pepper sauce *or* ¼ teaspoon red pepper flakes (optional)

¼ teaspoon salt

Discard seasoning packet.

1 Heat medium skillet over medium-high heat. Add noodles and sesame seeds; cook 2 minutes or until lightly browned, stirring frequently. Cool completely on plate.

2 Combine cabbage, carrots, onion and raisins in large bowl.

3 Place marmalade in medium microwavable bowl. Microwave on HIGH 30 seconds; stir until smooth. Whisk in vinegar, oil, ginger, soy sauce, orange peel, hot pepper sauce, if desired, and salt until well blended. Add to cabbage mixture; mix well. Cover and refrigerate at least 20 minutes.

4 Sprinkle with toasted noodles and sesame seed mixture before serving.

GINGER WONTON SOUP

MAKES 4 SERVINGS

4   ounces ground pork

½   cup ricotta cheese

1½ teaspoons minced fresh
    cilantro

½   teaspoon black pepper

¼   teaspoon salt

⅛   teaspoon Chinese
    five-spice powder

20 wonton wrappers

1   teaspoon vegetable oil

⅓   cup chopped red bell
    pepper

1   teaspoon grated fresh
    ginger or ginger paste

2   cans (about 14 ounces
    each) chicken broth

2   teaspoons soy sauce

4   ounces fresh snow peas

1   can (about 9 ounces)
    baby corn, rinsed and
    drained

2   green onions, thinly sliced

1 Cook pork in small nonstick skillet over medium-high heat 4 minutes or until no longer pink. Cool slightly; stir in ricotta, cilantro, black pepper, salt and five-spice powder.

2 Place 1 teaspoon filling in center of each wonton wrapper. Fold top corner of wonton over filling. Lightly brush remaining corners with water. Fold left and right corners over filling. Tightly roll up filled end toward remaining corner. Moisten edges with water to seal. Cover and set aside.

3 Heat oil in large saucepan over medium heat. Add bell pepper and ginger; cook 1 minute. Add broth and soy sauce; bring to a boil. Add snow peas, corn and wontons. Reduce heat to medium-low and simmer 4 to 5 minutes or until wontons are tender. Sprinkle with green onions.

SPICY GREEN BEANS

MAKES 4 SERVINGS

1 pound whole green
   beans, trimmed

2 tablespoons chopped
   green onions

2 tablespoons dry sherry
   or vegetable broth

4½ teaspoons soy sauce

1 teaspoon chili garlic sauce

1 teaspoon dark sesame oil

1 clove garlic, minced

1 Fill large saucepan with water to depth of ½ inch;
bring to a boil. Place green beans in steamer basket in
saucepan. Cover; steam about 5 minutes or just until
crisp-tender. Drain and set aside.

2 Combine green onions, sherry, soy sauce, chili sauce,
sesame oil and garlic in small bowl.

3 Spray saucepan with nonstick cooking spray; heat over
medium heat. Add green beans; pour soy sauce mixture
over beans. Toss well to coat. Cook 3 to 5 minutes or
until heated through, stirring constantly.

SPICY THAI COCONUT SOUP

MAKES 4 SERVINGS

2 cups chicken broth

1 can (about 13 ounces) coconut milk

1 tablespoon minced fresh ginger

1 teaspoon red curry paste

3 cups coarsely shredded cooked chicken (about 12 ounces)

1 can (15 ounces) straw mushrooms, drained

1 can (about 9 ounces) baby corn, drained

2 tablespoons lime juice

¼ cup chopped fresh cilantro

1 Bring broth, coconut milk, ginger and red curry paste to a simmer in large saucepan over medium heat.

2 Add chicken, mushrooms and corn; return to a simmer. Cook until heated through. Stir in lime juice. Sprinkle with cilantro just before serving.

NOTE: Red curry paste can be found in jars in the Asian food section of large grocery stores. Spice levels can vary among brands. Start with 1 teaspoon, then add more as desired.

MANDARIN CHICKEN SALAD

MAKES 4 SERVINGS

3½ ounces thin rice noodles (rice vermicelli)

1 can (6 ounces) mandarin orange segments, chilled

⅓ cup honey

2 tablespoons rice wine vinegar

2 tablespoons soy sauce

1 can (8 ounces) sliced water chestnuts, drained

4 cups shredded napa cabbage

1 cup shredded red cabbage

½ cup sliced radishes

4 thin slices red onion, cut in half and separated

3 boneless skinless chicken breasts (about 12 ounces), cooked and cut into strips

1 Place rice noodles in large bowl. Cover with hot water; soak 20 minutes or until soft. Drain.

2 Drain mandarin orange segments, reserving ⅓ cup liquid. Whisk reserved liquid, honey, vinegar and soy sauce in medium bowl. Add water chestnuts.

3 Divide noodles, cabbages, radishes and onion evenly among four serving plates. Top with chicken and orange segments. Remove water chestnuts from dressing and arrange on salads. Drizzle with remaining dressing.

TIP: To cook chicken, you can bake it, poach it, grill it or cook it in a skillet. Just be sure to cook it to 165°F and let it stand until it's cool enough to handle before cutting. Or cut up leftover rotisserie chicken to equal about 2 cups.

THAI COCONUT CHICKEN AND RICE SOUP

MAKES 6 TO 8 SERVINGS

1 pound boneless skinless chicken thighs, cut into 1-inch pieces

3 cups chicken broth

1 package (12 ounces) frozen chopped onions

1 can (4 ounces) sliced mushrooms, drained

2 tablespoons minced fresh ginger or ginger paste

2 tablespoons sugar

1 cup cooked rice

1 can (about 13 ounces) coconut milk

½ red bell pepper, thinly sliced

3 tablespoons chopped fresh cilantro

2 tablespoons grated lime peel

SLOW COOKER DIRECTIONS

1 Combine chicken, broth, onions, mushrooms, ginger and sugar in slow cooker. Cover and cook on LOW 8 to 9 hours.

2 Stir rice, coconut milk and bell pepper into soup. Cover and cook 15 minutes. Turn off heat. Stir in cilantro and lime peel just before serving.

TIP: To cook this soup in a saucepan, combine the ingredients in step 1 in a large saucepan instead of the slow cooker. Cover and cook over medium-low heat 30 minutes or until heated through. Proceed with step 2.

PORTOBELLO MUSHROOMS SESAME

MAKES 4 SERVINGS

4 large portobello
  mushrooms

2 tablespoons sweet rice
  wine or mirin

2 tablespoons soy sauce

2 cloves garlic, minced

1 teaspoon dark sesame oil

1 Prepare grill for direct cooking over medium heat.

2 Remove and discard stems from mushrooms; set caps aside. Whisk rice wine, soy sauce, garlic and sesame oil in small bowl until well blended.

3 Brush both sides of mushroom caps with soy sauce mixture. Grill, top sides up, covered, 3 to 4 minutes. Brush tops with soy sauce mixture; turn and grill 2 minutes or until grill marks appear. Turn again and grill, basting frequently, 4 to 5 minutes or until tender. Transfer to cutting board; cut diagonally into ½-inch-thick slices.

ASIAN FISH STEW

MAKES 4 TO 6 SERVINGS

8 dried black Chinese mushrooms

¼ cup soy sauce

2 tablespoons Chinese rice wine

1 teaspoon minced fresh ginger or ginger paste

Black pepper

8 ounces medium shrimp, peeled and deveined

8 ounces halibut, cubed

1 tablespoon vegetable oil

2 cloves garlic, chopped

2 cups sliced bok choy

1½ cups sliced napa cabbage

1 cup broccoli florets

2 cups chicken broth

½ cup bottled clam juice or water

2 tablespoons water

2 tablespoons cornstarch

4 ounces pea pods, stems removed

2 green onions, sliced

Hot cooked rice (optional)

1 Place mushrooms in medium bowl; cover with hot water. Soak about 30 minutes or until soft. Cut off and discard stems; thinly caps.

2 Whisk soy sauce, rice wine and ginger in medium bowl until well blended; season with pepper. Add shrimp and halibut; marinate at room temperature 10 minutes.

3 Meanwhile, heat oil in Dutch oven or large saucepan over medium-high heat. Add garlic; cook and stir 30 seconds or until fragrant. Stir in bok choy, cabbage and broccoli.

4 Drain seafood, reserving marinade. Add broth, clam juice and reserved marinade to Dutch oven; bring to a boil over high heat. Reduce heat to low; simmer 5 to 10 minutes until vegetables are crisp-tender. Add seafood and mushrooms; simmer 3 to 5 minutes until shrimp are opaque and fish flakes easily when tested with fork.

5 Stir water into cornstarch in small bowl until smooth; stir into soup. Cook and stir until stew boils and thickens slightly. Remove from heat; stir in pea pods and green onions. Serve with rice, if desired.

CHINESE CRAB AND CUCUMBER SALAD

MAKES 4 TO 6 SERVINGS

1 large cucumber, peeled

12 ounces crabmeat (fresh, pasteurized or thawed frozen), flaked

½ red bell pepper, diced

½ cup mayonnaise

3 tablespoons soy sauce

1 tablespoon dark sesame oil

1 teaspoon ground ginger

8 ounces bean sprouts

1 tablespoon sesame seeds, toasted*

Chopped fresh chives

To toast sesame seeds, spread seeds in small skillet. Shake skillet over medium heat about 1 minute until seeds begin to pop and turn golden.

1 Cut cucumber in half lengthwise; scoop out seeds. Cut crosswise into ½-inch slices.

2 Combine cucumber, crabmeat and bell pepper in large bowl. Whisk mayonnaise, soy sauce, sesame oil and ginger in small bowl until blended. Add to crabmeat mixture; toss gently to coat. Cover and refrigerate 1 hour to allow flavors to blend.

3 To serve, arrange bean sprouts on individual serving plates. Spoon crabmeat mixture over sprouts; sprinkle with sesame seeds and chives.

BRAISED CABBAGE

MAKES 6 SERVINGS

½ small head green cabbage (about 8 ounces)

1 small head bok choy

½ cup vegetable broth

2 tablespoons rice wine vinegar

2 tablespoons soy sauce

1 tablespoon packed brown sugar

¼ teaspoon red pepper flakes (optional)

1 tablespoon water

1 tablespoon cornstarch

1 Cut cabbage into 1-inch pieces. Trim and discard bottoms from bok choy; slice stems into ½-inch pieces. Cut tops of leaves into ½-inch slices; set aside.

2 Combine cabbage and bok choy stems in large nonstick skillet. Add broth, vinegar, soy sauce, brown sugar and red pepper flakes, if desired.

3 Bring to a boil over high heat. Reduce heat to medium. Cover and simmer 5 minutes or until vegetables are crisp-tender.

4 Stir water into cornstarch in small bowl until smooth. Stir into skillet. Cook and stir 1 minute or until sauce boils and thickens.

5 Stir in reserved bok choy leaves; cook 1 minute.

THAI CURRIED VEGETABLES

MAKES 4 TO 6 SERVINGS

1   can (about 13 ounces) coconut milk

1   tablespoon Thai red curry paste

1   bag (16 ounces) frozen Asian vegetable mixture, such as broccoli, carrots and water chestnuts

½   teaspoon salt

    Hot cooked rice (optional)

1 Combine coconut milk and curry paste in large saucepan. Cook and stir over medium-high heat 5 minutes.

2 Add vegetables and salt; bring to a boil. Reduce heat to medium; cover and cook until vegetables are crisp-tender, stirring occasionally. Serve over rice, if desired.

EXTRAS: Add bite-size pieces of boneless skinless chicken or cubes of tofu to coconut milk mixture and simmer until chicken is cooked through. Serve over hot cooked rice. Garnish with slivered fresh basil.

JAPANESE EGG DROP SOUP

MAKES 4 SERVINGS

4 ounces boneless skinless chicken breast, cut into 1½×½-inch pieces

1 teaspoon sake

¾ teaspoon salt, divided

¾ cup water

1 (1-inch) piece carrot, cut into ⅛-inch-thick slices

4 cups fish stock

1 teaspoon soy sauce

2 eggs, lightly beaten

1 Combine chicken, sake and ¼ teaspoon salt in small bowl; set aside.

2 Bring water and ¼ teaspoon salt to a boil in small saucepan over medium heat. Add carrot slices; cook 2 minutes. Drain.

3 Bring stock to a boil in medium saucepan over medium-high heat. Add remaining ¼ teaspoon salt, soy sauce and chicken. Reduce heat to medium; boil 2 minutes.

4 Slowly pour about one third of eggs at a time into boiling soup, stirring constantly. Return soup to a boil after each addition. Remove from heat immediately after last egg "threads" form.

5 Place 2 carrot slices in each of 4 individual soup bowls. Ladle about 1 cup soup over carrots in each bowl.

CASHEW GREEN BEANS

MAKES 4 SERVINGS

1 tablespoon peanut or vegetable oil

1 small onion, halved and thinly sliced

2 cloves garlic, minced

1 package (10 ounces) frozen julienne-cut green beans, thawed, drained and patted dry

2 tablespoons oyster sauce

1 tablespoon rice vinegar

1 tablespoon honey

¼ cup coarsely chopped cashews or peanuts

1 Heat oil in wok or large skillet over medium-high heat. Add onion and garlic; stir-fry 3 minutes. Add green beans; stir-fry 2 minutes.

2 Add oyster sauce, vinegar and honey; stir-fry 1 minute or until heated through. Remove from heat; stir in cashews. Serve immediately.

FROM THE WOK

CHICKEN CHOW MEIN

MAKES 4 SERVINGS

1 pound boneless skinless chicken breasts or thighs

2 cloves garlic, minced

2 tablespoons peanut or vegetable oil, divided

¼ cup soy sauce

2 tablespoons dry sherry

6 ounces (2 cups) fresh snow peas *or* 1 package (6 ounces) frozen snow peas, thawed, cut into halves

3 green onions, cut diagonally into 1-inch pieces

6 ounces uncooked Chinese egg noodles or vermicelli, cooked, drained and rinsed

1 tablespoon dark sesame oil

1 Cut chicken crosswise into ¼-inch slices; cut each slice into 1×¼-inch strips. Toss chicken with garlic in medium bowl.

2 Heat 1 tablespoon peanut oil in wok or large skillet over medium-high heat. Add chicken mixture; stir-fry 3 minutes or until chicken is no longer pink. Remove to large bowl; toss with soy sauce and sherry.

3 Heat remaining 1 tablespoon peanut oil in wok. Add snow peas; stir-fry 2 minutes for fresh snow peas or 1 minute for frozen. Add green onions; stir-fry 30 seconds. Add chicken mixture; stir-fry 1 minute.

4 Add noodles to wok; stir-fry 2 minutes or until heated through. Stir in sesame oil. Serve immediately.

FUKIEN RED-COOKED PORK

MAKES 4 TO 5 SERVINGS

5¼ cups plus 3 tablespoons water, divided

2 pounds boneless pork shoulder, well trimmed, cut into 1½-inch chunks

⅓ cup rice wine or dry sherry

⅓ cup soy sauce

¼ cup packed brown sugar

1 piece fresh ginger (about 1½ inches), peeled and cut into strips

3 cloves garlic, chopped

1 teaspoon anise seeds

1 pound carrots, diagonally sliced

2 tablespoons cornstarch

½ head napa cabbage (about 1 pound), core removed, cut into 1-inch slices

1 teaspoon dark sesame oil

Hot cooked rice (optional)

1 Place 4 cups water in wok; bring to a boil over high heat. Add pork; return to a boil and cook 2 minutes. Drain in colander; return pork to wok. Add remaining 1¼ cups water, wine, soy sauce, brown sugar, ginger, garlic and anise. Cover; bring to a boil. Reduce heat to low; simmer 1¼ hours or until meat is almost tender, stirring occasionally.

2 Add carrots to wok; cover and cook 20 minutes or until pork and carrots are fork-tender. Transfer to serving bowl with slotted spoon.

3 Stir remaining 3 tablespoons water into cornstarch in small bowl until smooth.

4 Add cabbage to liquid in wok. Cover and increase heat to medium-high. Cook cabbage about 2 minutes or until wilted. Stir cornstarch mixture; add to cabbage. Cook until sauce boils and thickens. Return pork and carrots to wok; add oil and mix well. Serve with rice, if desired.

NOTE: "Red cooking" is a Chinese cooking method in which meat or poultry is braised in soy sauce, giving the meat a deep, rich color.

SIMPLE FRIED RICE

MAKES 6 SERVINGS

2 tablespoons vegetable oil

3 green onions, chopped

2 eggs, lightly beaten

3 cups cooked rice, cold or
at room temperature

4 ounces cooked shrimp,
chicken, ham, beef or
pork, chopped

3 tablespoons soy sauce

1 Heat wok or large skillet over medium heat. Add oil;
heat until oil shimmers. Add green onions; cook and stir
about 30 seconds. Pour in eggs, stirring constantly until
cooked.

2 Add rice; cook and stir 2 to 3 minutes or until heated
through. Stir in shrimp and soy sauce; cook and stir
1 to 2 minutes or until heated through.

VARIATION: Use tofu or cooked vegetables in place of
shrimp or meat.

FIVE-SPICE BEEF AND BOK CHOY

MAKES 4 SERVINGS

1 boneless beef top sirloin steak (about 1 pound)

¼ cup soy sauce

2 tablespoons dry sherry

2 teaspoons minced fresh ginger or ginger paste

2 cloves garlic, minced

1 teaspoon sugar

½ teaspoon Chinese five-spice powder

¼ teaspoon red pepper flakes (optional)

1 large head bok choy

2 teaspoons cornstarch

2 tablespoons peanut oil or vegetable oil, divided

Hot cooked rice

Honey roasted peanuts (optional)

1 Trim fat from beef; discard. Cut beef lengthwise in half, then crosswise into ⅛-inch-thick slices. Combine soy sauce, sherry, ginger, garlic, sugar, five-spice powder and red pepper flakes, if desired, in medium bowl. Add beef and toss to coat; set aside.

2 Separate bok choy leaves from stems; rinse and pat dry. Stack leaves and cut crosswise into 1-inch slices. Cut stems diagonally into ½-inch slices. Keep leaves and stems separate.

3 Drain beef, reserving marinade. Stir reserved marinade into cornstarch in small bowl; stir until smooth. Set aside.

4 Heat wok over medium-high heat. Drizzle 1 tablespoon oil into wok and heat 30 seconds. Add half of beef; stir-fry 2 minutes or until beef is barely pink in center. Remove beef from wok; set aside. Repeat with remaining beef.

5 Add remaining 1 tablespoon oil and heat 30 seconds. Add bok choy stems; stir-fry 3 minutes. Add bok choy leaves; stir-fry 2 minutes.

6 Stir marinade mixture until smooth; add to wok. Stir-fry until sauce boils for 1 minute and thickens.

7 Return beef and any accumulated juices to wok; cook until heated through. Serve over rice; garnish with peanuts.

THAI BASIL PORK STIR-FRY

MAKES 6 SERVINGS

1 pound pork tenderloin, sliced across the grain into ¼-inch slices

1 tablespoon soy sauce

½ teaspoon minced garlic

2 tablespoons canola oil

1 broccoli crown, cut into florets

1 medium red bell pepper, cut into strips

1 to 2 tablespoons Thai green curry paste*

1¼ cups chicken broth

2 tablespoons chopped fresh basil

2 tablespoons finely chopped roasted peanuts

3 cups fresh mung bean sprouts

Thai green curry paste is available in the ethnic section of most supermarkets in cans or jars. Use 1 tablespoon for a mildly spicy dish or 2 tablespoons for a hot dish.

1 Combine pork, soy sauce and garlic in medium bowl; toss to coat.

2 Heat oil in work or large nonstick skillet over high heat. Add broccoli; stir-fry 3 to 4 minutes or until broccoli begins to brown. Add bell pepper; stir-fry 1 minute. Add pork mixture and curry paste; stir-fry 2 minutes. Add broth; cook and stir 2 to 3 minutes or until heated through.

3 Remove from heat; stir in chopped basil. Sprinkle with peanuts and serve with bean sprouts.

CASHEW CHICKEN

MAKES 4 SERVINGS

10 ounces boneless skinless chicken breasts, cut into 1×½-inch pieces

1 tablespoon cornstarch

1 tablespoon dry white wine

1 tablespoon soy sauce

½ teaspoon garlic powder

1 teaspoon vegetable oil

6 green onions, cut into 1-inch pieces

2 cups sliced white mushrooms

1 red or green bell pepper, cut into strips

1 can (6 ounces) sliced water chestnuts, rinsed and drained

2 tablespoons hoisin sauce (optional)

Hot cooked white rice

¼ cup cashews, toasted*

To toast cashews, spread in single layer in heavy-bottomed skillet. Cook over medium heat 2 to 3 minutes, stirring frequently, until nuts are lightly browned. Cool before using.

1 Place chicken in large resealable food storage bag. Whisk cornstarch, wine, soy sauce and garlic powder in small bowl until smooth and well blended. Pour over chicken. Seal bag; turn to coat. Marinate in refrigerator 1 hour.

2 Drain chicken; discard marinade. Heat oil in wok or large nonstick skillet over medium-high heat. Add green onions; cook and stir 1 minute. Add chicken; cook and stir 2 minutes or until browned.

3 Add mushrooms, bell pepper and water chestnuts; cook and stir 3 minutes or until vegetables are crisp-tender and chicken is cooked through. Stir in hoisin sauce, if desired; cook and stir 1 minute or until heated through.

4 Serve chicken and vegetables over rice. Top with cashews.

didn't add hoisn sauce - VERY Hard

FRIED TOFU WITH ASIAN VEGETABLES

MAKES 6 SERVINGS

1 package (14 to 16 ounces) firm tofu

½ cup soy sauce, divided

1 cup all-purpose flour

¾ teaspoon salt, divided

⅛ teaspoon black pepper

Vegetable oil for frying

2 packages (16 ounces each) frozen mixed Asian vegetables*

3 tablespoons water

1 teaspoon cornstarch

3 tablespoons plum sauce

2 tablespoons lemon juice

2 teaspoons sugar

1 teaspoon minced fresh ginger

⅛ to ¼ teaspoon red pepper flakes

Frozen vegetables do not need to be thawed before cooking.

1 Drain tofu; cut into ¾-inch cubes. Gently mix tofu and ¼ cup soy sauce in shallow bowl; let stand 5 minutes. Combine flour, ½ teaspoon salt and black pepper in medium bowl. Working in batches, toss tofu in flour mixture to coat.

2 Heat 1½ inches oil in wok or Dutch oven. Test heat by dropping 1 tofu cube into oil; it should brown in 1 minute. Fry tofu cubes in small batches until browned. Remove from oil with slotted spoon and drain on paper towels.

3 Pour off all but 1 tablespoon oil from wok. Add frozen vegetables and remaining ¼ teaspoon salt. Cook over medium-high heat about 6 minutes or until vegetables are heated through, stirring occasionally. Increase heat to high to evaporate any remaining liquid. Set aside; cover to keep warm.

4 Stir water into cornstarch in small bowl until well blended. Combine cornstarch mixture, remaining ¼ cup soy sauce, plum sauce, lemon juice, sugar, ginger and red pepper flakes in small saucepan; cook and stir over low heat 1 to 2 minutes or until sauce is slightly thickened; stir to mix well. Spoon vegetables into serving bowl. Top with tofu and sauce; toss gently to mix.

CHICKEN STIR-FRY WITH CABBAGE PANCAKE

MAKES 4 SERVINGS

2 cups shredded coleslaw mix

2 eggs, lightly beaten

1 teaspoon soy sauce

½ teaspoon white pepper

2 teaspoons vegetable oil, divided

1 pound fresh asparagus, trimmed, cut into 1-inch pieces

1 package (8 ounces) sliced mushrooms

1 pound boneless skinless chicken breast tenders, cut into 1-inch pieces

1 teaspoon grated fresh ginger or ginger paste, divided

1 teaspoon minced garlic, divided

1 teaspoon dark sesame oil, divided

½ cup water

1 tablespoon cornstarch

1 For pancake, combine coleslaw mix, eggs, soy sauce and white pepper in large bowl until well blended. Heat 1 teaspoon vegetable oil in 12-inch nonstick skillet over medium-high heat. Pour coleslaw mixture into skillet; pat into even layer. Cover and cook about 4 minutes or until set and browned. Turn pancake and cook, uncovered, about 2 minutes. Transfer to plate; keep warm.

2 For stir-fry, heat remaining 1 teaspoon vegetable oil in wok or same skillet over medium-high heat. Add asparagus; stir-fry 1 to 2 minutes. Add mushrooms; stir-fry 2 minutes. Add chicken, ½ teaspoon ginger, ½ teaspoon garlic and ½ teaspoon sesame oil; stir-fry 3 minutes or until chicken is cooked through.

3 Stir water, cornstarch, remaining ginger, garlic and sesame oil in small bowl until well blended. Add to wok; cook and stir 1 to 2 minutes or until sauce thickens slightly.

4 Cut pancake into 4 wedges. Spoon stir-fry over each wedge.

THAI GREEN CURRY

MAKES 2 TO 4 SERVINGS

1 onion, chopped

1 tablespoon vegetable oil

1 package (14 to 16 ounces) firm tofu, drained and cut into 1-inch cubes

⅓ cup Thai green curry paste

1 can (about 13 ounces) coconut milk

1 broccoli crown, cut into florets

1 cup cut green beans (1-inch pieces)

½ teaspoon salt

Hot cooked brown rice or rice noodles

1 Heat oil in large skillet or wok over high heat. Add onion; cook and stir 5 minutes or until onion is soft and lightly browned.

2 Add tofu and curry paste; cook and stir 2 minutes or until curry is fragrant and tofu is coated. Add coconut milk; bring to a boil. Reduce heat to low. Add broccoli and green beans.

3 Cook 20 minutes or until vegetables are tender and sauce is thickened, stirring frequently. Taste and season with salt. Serve over rice.

VERMICELLI WITH PORK

MAKES 4 SERVINGS

4   ounces Chinese rice vermicelli or bean threads

32 dried mushrooms

3   green onions with tops, divided

2   tablespoons minced fresh ginger or ginger paste

2   tablespoons hot bean sauce

1½ cups chicken broth

1   tablespoon dry sherry

1   tablespoon soy sauce

2   tablespoons vegetable oil

6   ounces ground pork

1   small red or green hot chile pepper, seeded and finely chopped*

Hot chile peppers are deceptively potent. Wear rubber or plastic gloves when removing seeds or chopping peppers and do not touch your eyes or lips when handling.

1 Place vermicelli and dried mushrooms in separate large bowls; cover each with hot water. Let stand 30 minutes; drain. Cut vermicelli into 4-inch pieces.

2 Squeeze out as much excess water as possible from mushrooms. Cut off and discard mushroom stems; thinly slice caps.

3 Cut 1 green onion into 1½-inch slivers; reserve for garnish. Thinly slice remaining 2 green onions.

4 Combine ginger and hot bean sauce in small bowl. Combine broth, sherry and soy sauce in another small bowl.

5 Heat oil in wok or large skillet over high heat. Add pork; stir-fry about 2 minutes or until no longer pink. Add chile pepper, sliced onions and bean sauce mixture; stir-fry 1 minute.

6 Add broth mixture, vermicelli and mushrooms. Simmer, uncovered, about 5 minutes until most of liquid is absorbed. Top with reserved green onions.

PINEAPPLE BASIL CHICKEN SUPREME

MAKES 4 SERVINGS

1 can (8 ounces) pineapple chunks in unsweetened juice

2 teaspoons cornstarch

2 tablespoons peanut oil

1 pound boneless skinless chicken breasts, cut into ¾-inch pieces

2 serrano peppers, cut into thin strips (optional)

2 cloves garlic, minced

2 green onions, cut into 1-inch pieces

¾ cup roasted cashews

¼ cup chopped fresh basil

1 tablespoon fish sauce

1 tablespoon soy sauce

Hot cooked rice (optional)

1 Drain pineapple, reserving juice. Combine reserved juice and cornstarch in small bowl until well blended; set aside.

2 Heat wok or large skillet over high heat 1 minute. Drizzle oil into wok; heat 30 seconds. Add chicken, peppers, if desired, and garlic; stir-fry 3 minutes or until chicken is cooked through. Add green onions; stir-fry 1 minute.

3 Stir cornstarch mixture; add to wok. Cook and stir 1 minute or until thickened. Add pineapple, cashews, basil, fish sauce and soy sauce; cook and stir 1 minute or until heated through. Serve over rice, if desired.

SESAME BEEF WITH PINEAPPLE-PLUM SAUCE

MAKES 4 SERVINGS

1 beef flank steak (about 1 pound)

3 tablespoons soy sauce, divided

3½ teaspoons cornstarch, divided

2 teaspoons grated fresh ginger or ginger paste

2 cloves garlic, minced

⅛ teaspoon red pepper flakes

1 package (12 ounces) fresh refrigerated pineapple spears or chunks*

1 tablespoon sesame seeds

1 tablespoon vegetable oil

¼ cup chicken broth

¼ cup minced green onions, green parts only, plus additional for garnish

¼ cup thin red bell pepper slices

2 tablespoons plum sauce

Fresh pineapple spears packed in plastic containers can be found in supermarket produce departments. If unavailable, use 1½ cups canned pineapple chunks packed in unsweetened juice.

1 Cut steak lengthwise in half, then across the grain into thin slices. Stir 2 tablespoons soy sauce into 1½ teaspoons cornstarch in medium bowl until well blended. Add steak, ginger, garlic and red pepper flakes; toss to coat. Let stand 30 minutes.

2 Drain pineapple, reserving juice. Stir 2 tablespoons pineapple juice into remaining 2 teaspoons cornstarch in small bowl; mix well. Cut pineapple spears into chunks.

3 Toast sesame seeds in small skillet over medium-low heat about 3 minutes or until golden. Immediately remove from skillet; set aside.

4 Heat oil in wok over medium-high heat. Working in batches, brown beef 2 minutes per side or until beef is barely pink in center.

5 Stir cornstarch mixture; add to wok with broth, ¼ cup green onions and bell pepper, plum sauce and remaining 1 tablespoon soy sauce. Cook and stir 1 minute or until sauce thickens. Stir in pineapple chunks; cook and stir until heated through. Sprinkle with sesame seeds; garnish with additional green onions.

BEAN THREADS WITH MINCED PORK

MAKES 4 SERVINGS

4 ounces bean threads or Chinese rice vermicelli

3 dried mushrooms

2 tablespoons minced fresh ginger or ginger paste

2 tablespoons chile black bean sauce

1½ cups chicken broth

1 tablespoon soy sauce

1 tablespoon dry sherry

2 tablespoons vegetable oil

6 ounces ground pork

1 small red or green hot chile pepper, seeded and minced

2 green onions, thinly sliced

1 Place bean threads and dried mushrooms in separate bowls. Cover each with hot water. Let stand 30 minutes; drain. Cut bean threads into 4-inch pieces. Squeeze out excess water from mushrooms. Cut off and discard stems; thinly slice caps.

2 Combine ginger and bean sauce in small bowl. Combine broth, soy sauce and sherry in medium bowl.

3 Heat oil in wok or large skillet over high heat. Add pork; stir-fry about 2 minutes or until pork is no longer pink. Add chile pepper, green onions and bean sauce mixture. Stir-fry until pork absorbs color from bean sauce, about 1 minute.

4 Add broth mixture, bean threads and mushrooms. Simmer, uncovered, about 5 minutes until most liquid is absorbed.

BUDDHA'S DELIGHT

MAKES 2 TO 4 SERVINGS

1 package (1 ounce) dried black Chinese mushrooms

1 package (14 to 16 ounces) firm tofu, drained

1 tablespoon peanut or vegetable oil

2 cups diagonally cut 1-inch asparagus pieces

1 medium onion, halved and thinly sliced

2 cloves garlic, minced

½ cup vegetable broth

3 tablespoons hoisin sauce

¼ cup coarsely chopped fresh cilantro or thinly sliced green onions

1 Place mushrooms in medium bowl; cover with hot water. Soak 30 minutes or until soft. Drain mushrooms, reserving soaking liquid. Cut off and discard stems; thinly slice caps.

2 Meanwhile, place tofu on plate or cutting board lined with paper towels. Cover with additional paper towels and place flat, heavy object on top. Let stand 15 minutes. Cut tofu into ¾-inch cubes or triangles.

3 Heat oil in wok or large skillet over medium-high heat. Add asparagus, onion and garlic; stir-fry 4 minutes.

4 Add mushrooms, ¼ cup reserved mushroom liquid, broth and hoisin sauce; cook over medium-low heat 1 to 2 minutes or until asparagus is crisp-tender.

5 Stir in tofu; heat through. Ladle into shallow bowls; sprinkle with cilantro.

CHICKEN FRIED RICE

MAKES 4 SERVINGS

2   tablespoons vegetable oil, divided

12 ounces boneless skinless chicken breasts, cut into ½-inch cubes

    Salt and black pepper

2   tablespoons butter

2   cloves garlic, minced

½   sweet onion, diced

1   medium carrot, diced

2   green onions, thinly sliced

3   eggs

4   cups cooked white rice*

3   tablespoons soy sauce

2   tablespoons sesame seeds

For rice, cook 1½ cups white rice according to package directions without oil or butter. Spread hot rice on large rimmed baking sheet; cool to room temperature. Refrigerate several hours or overnight. Measure 4 cups.

1 Heat 1 tablespoon oil in wok or large skillet over medium-high heat. Add chicken; season with salt and pepper. Cook and stir 5 to 6 minutes or until cooked through. Add butter and garlic; cook and stir 1 minute or until butter is melted. Transfer to medium bowl.

2 Add onion, carrot and green onions to wok; cook and stir over high heat 3 minutes or until vegetables are softened. Add to bowl with chicken.

3 Heat remaining 1 tablespoon oil in wok. Crack eggs into wok; cook and stir 45 seconds or until eggs are scrambled but still moist. Add chicken and vegetable mixture, rice, soy sauce and sesame seeds; cook and stir 2 minutes or until well blended and heated through. Season with salt and pepper to taste.

BOWLS

CHICKEN CONGEE
MAKES 6 SERVINGS

6 cups water

4 cups chicken broth

4 chicken drumsticks

1 cup uncooked white jasmine rice, rinsed and drained

1 (1-inch) piece ginger, peeled and cut into 4 slices

2 teaspoons kosher salt

¼ teaspoon ground white pepper

Toppings: soy sauce, dark sesame oil, thinly sliced green onions, fried shallots, fried garlic slices, salted roasted peanuts, pickled ginger and/or thinly sliced vegetables

SLOW COOKER DIRECTIONS

1 Combine water, broth, chicken, rice, ginger, salt and pepper in slow cooker. Cover; cook on LOW 8 hours or on HIGH 4 hours or until rice has completely broken down and mixture is thickened.

2 Remove and discard ginger. Transfer chicken to large cutting board. Discard skin and bones. Shred chicken using two forks. Stir chicken back into slow cooker. Ladle congee into serving bowls; top with desired toppings.

CALIFORNIA ROLL FARRO SUSHI BOWL

MAKES 4 SERVINGS

BOWL

- 1 package (8½ ounces) quick-cooking farro *or* 1 cup uncooked regular farro
- 2 tablespoons rice vinegar
- 2 tablespoons sugar
- ½ teaspoon salt
- 1 cup shredded carrots
- 2 avocados, sliced
- 2 mini (kirby) cucumbers, thinly sliced
- 12 ounces crab sticks or imitation crab sticks
- 2 teaspoons toasted sesame seeds

SAUCE

- ⅓ cup mayonnaise
- 1 teaspoon sriracha sauce
- 1 teaspoon dark sesame oil
- 1 teaspoon rice vinegar

1 Prepare farro according to package directions.

2 Combine 2 tablespoons rice vinegar, sugar and salt in large microwavable bowl; microwave on HIGH 30 to 45 seconds or until sugar is dissolved. Stir mixture; add farro and toss to coat.

3 Divide farro mixture evenly among 4 bowls. Top with carrots, avocado, cucumbers and crab sticks. Sprinkle with sesame seeds.

4 For sauce, whisk mayonnaise, sriracha sauce, sesame oil and 1 teaspoon rice vinegar in small bowl until well blended. Serve with bowls.

THAI RED CURRY WITH TOFU

MAKES 4 SERVINGS

1 medium sweet potato, peeled and cut into 1-inch pieces

1 small eggplant or large zucchini, halved lengthwise and cut crosswise into ½-inch-wide slices

8 ounces extra firm tofu, cut into 1-inch pieces

½ cup green bean pieces (1-inch pieces)

½ red bell pepper, cut into ¼-inch strips

2 tablespoons vegetable oil

5 medium shallots, thinly sliced (1½ cups)

3 tablespoons Thai red curry paste

1 teaspoon minced garlic

1 teaspoon grated fresh ginger or ginger paste

1 can (about 13 ounces) coconut milk

1½ tablespoons soy sauce

1 tablespoon packed brown sugar

¼ cup chopped fresh basil

2 tablespoons lime juice

Hot cooked rice (optional)

SLOW COOKER DIRECTIONS

1 Coat inside of slow cooker with nonstick cooking spray. Add potato, eggplant, tofu, beans and bell pepper.

2 Heat oil in large skillet over medium heat. Add shallots; cook 5 minutes or until browned and tender. Add curry paste, garlic and ginger; cook and stir 1 minute. Add coconut milk, soy sauce and brown sugar; bring to a simmer. Pour mixture over vegetables in slow cooker.

3 Cover; cook on LOW 2 to 3 hours. Stir in basil and lime juice. Serve over rice, if desired.

THREE-TOPPED RICE

MAKES 4 SERVINGS

2½ cups uncooked short-grain rice

4¼ cups water, divided

1 teaspoon salt, divided

1½ cups fresh or frozen green peas

1 piece fresh ginger (about 1-inch square), grated *or* 1 tablespoon ginger paste

2 tablespoons sugar, divided

2 tablespoons sake or dry sherry, divided

1 tablespoon plus 1 teaspoon soy sauce, divided

8 ounces ground chicken

4 eggs, lightly beaten

Pickled ginger*

*Available in Asian grocery stores and the Asian aisle of large grocery stores. Sometimes it is labeled sushi ginger.

1 Place rice in large bowl; add cold water to cover. Stir rice gently with fingers. (Water will become cloudy.) Drain rice in colander. Repeat washing and draining 3 or 4 times until water remains almost clear. Place rice in large heavy saucepan with tight-fitting lid. Add 2¾ cups water; soak 30 minutes. Stir ½ teaspoon salt into rice. Cover and bring to a boil over medium-high heat. Reduce heat to low; simmer 15 minutes or until liquid is absorbed. *Do not lift lid during cooking.* Remove pan from heat; let stand, covered, 15 minutes. Gently fluff rice with wooden spoon or paddle. Lay dry kitchen towel over saucepan; cover towel with lid. Let stand 10 minutes to absorb excess moisture.

2 Place peas, remaining 1½ cups water and ½ teaspoon salt in small saucepan. Bring to a boil over medium-high heat; boil 4 minutes or until peas are tender. Drain well. Squeeze grated ginger between thumb and fingers to extract juice into cup. Squeeze enough ginger to measure 1 teaspoon ginger juice. Combine 1 tablespoon sugar, 1 tablespoon sake, 1 tablespoon soy sauce and ginger juice in medium saucepan; bring to a boil over high heat. Add chicken; cook and stir 3 to 4 minutes or until chicken is no longer pink. Turn off heat.

3 Place eggs, remaining 1 tablespoon sugar, 1 tablespoon sake and 1 teaspoon soy sauce in medium skillet. Cook 3 to 5 minutes over medium-low heat until eggs are set but still moist, stirring constantly. Remove from heat.

4 Divide rice among 4 serving bowls. Top with chicken, peas, eggs and pickled ginger.

CHICKEN RAMEN NOODLE BOWLS

MAKES 6 SERVINGS

1 tablespoon olive oil

1 pound boneless skinless chicken thighs

1 large yellow onion, peeled and halved

6 cups chicken broth

2 tablespoons soy sauce

4 green onions, divided

1 (1-inch) piece fresh ginger, sliced

1 clove garlic

6 ounces shiitake mushrooms, thinly sliced

⅓ cup hoisin sauce

8 ounces uncooked fresh Chinese noodles

3 hard-cooked eggs, cut in half lengthwise

¼ cup thinly sliced red bell pepper

Chopped fresh cilantro

SLOW COOKER DIRECTIONS

1 Heat oil in large skillet over medium-high heat. Add chicken; cook 8 to 10 minutes or until browned. Transfer to slow cooker using slotted spoon. Add onion halves to skillet, cut side down; cook 4 to 5 minutes or until lightly charred. Transfer to slow cooker. Add broth, soy sauce, 2 green onions, ginger and garlic to slow cooker.

2 Cover; cook on LOW 6 to 7 hours or on HIGH 3 to 4 hours or until chicken is tender. Transfer chicken to large cutting board; shred with two forks. Strain broth into large bowl. Discard solids; return broth to slow cooker. Stir in mushrooms and hoisin sauce. Cover; cook on HIGH 30 minutes.

3 Divide noodles and broth evenly among 6 bowls. Top with chicken, mushrooms, one egg half, bell pepper and cilantro. Chop remaining 2 green onions; sprinkle over bowls.

TOFU SATAY BOWL

MAKES 4 SERVINGS

1 package (14 to 16 ounces) firm or extra firm tofu, drained and pressed*

⅓ cup water

⅓ cup soy sauce

1 tablespoon dark sesame oil

1 teaspoon minced garlic

1 teaspoon minced fresh ginger or ginger paste

16 to 24 white or cremini mushrooms, trimmed

1 red bell pepper, cut into 24 pieces

Cucumber Relish (recipe follows)

PEANUT SAUCE

1 can (about 13 ounces) coconut milk

½ cup creamy peanut butter

2 tablespoons packed brown sugar

1 tablespoon rice vinegar

2 teaspoons Thai red curry paste

1 cup uncooked jasmine rice, cooked according to package directions

If you use extra firm silken tofu, there is no need to press it.

1 Cut tofu into 24 cubes. Combine water, soy sauce, sesame oil, garlic and ginger in small bowl. Place tofu, mushrooms and bell pepper in large resealable food storage bag. Add soy sauce mixture. Seal bag; turn to coat. Marinate 30 minutes, turning occasionally. Soak eight 8-inch bamboo skewers in cold water 20 minutes. Meanwhile, prepare cucumber relish.

2 Preheat oven to 400°F. Spray 13×9-inch baking pan with nonstick cooking spray. Drain tofu mixture; discard marinade. Thread tofu and vegetables alternately onto skewers; place in prepared baking pan. Bake 25 minutes or until tofu cubes are lightly browned and vegetables are softened.

3 Meanwhile, whisk coconut milk, peanut butter, brown sugar, vinegar and curry paste in small saucepan over medium heat. Bring to a boil, stirring constantly. Immediately reduce heat to low. Cook about 20 minutes or until creamy and thick, stirring frequently. Serve tofu, vegetables and sauce over rice with cucumber relish.

CUCUMBER RELISH: Cook ¼ cup rice vinegar, 2 tablespoons granulated sugar and ¼ teaspoon salt in small saucepan over medium heat until sugar is dissolved. Pour into large bowl; cool completely. Stir in 1 medium cucumber, halved and thinly sliced, ½ red onion, halved and thinly sliced, and 1 large carrot, peeled and shredded. Serve immediately or refrigerate until ready to serve.

NOODLES

PEANUT NOODLES
MAKES 4 SERVINGS

3 tablespoons vegetable oil, divided

2 tablespoons peanut butter

1 tablespoon teriyaki sauce

Juice of 1 lime

1 teaspoon chili garlic paste (optional)

2 packages (3 ounces each) ramen noodles, any flavor*

¾ cup shelled edamame, thawed if frozen

½ cup thinly sliced red bell pepper

Chopped peanuts (optional)

Discard seasoning packets.

1 Whisk 2 tablespoons oil, peanut butter, teriyaki sauce, lime juice and chili garlic paste, if desired, in small bowl until smooth.

2 Bring water to a boil in large saucepan over medium-high heat. Add noodles and edamame; boil 2 minutes. Drain and rinse under cold water until cool. Place in large bowl. Add remaining 1 tablespoon oil; toss to coat.

3 Add bell pepper and sauce; toss to coat. Top with peanuts, if desired.

QUICK CHICKEN AND CABBAGE SESAME NOODLES

MAKES 6 SERVINGS

8 ounces whole wheat or regular spaghetti

2 tablespoons rice vinegar

2 tablespoons soy sauce

2 tablespoons water

1½ tablespoons dark sesame oil

1 tablespoon dark brown sugar

2 cups (about 16 ounces) shredded cooked chicken

1½ cups chopped red cabbage

⅓ cup chopped green onion

¼ cup chopped peanuts

3 tablespoons chopped fresh cilantro

1 Cook spaghetti according to package directions. Drain.

2 Whisk vinegar, soy sauce, water, oil and brown sugar in large bowl.

3 Add spaghetti, chicken, cabbage and green onion; toss to coat. Top each serving with peanuts and cilantro.

VEGETABLE LO MEIN
MAKES 4 SERVINGS

8 ounces uncooked
   Chinese egg noodles
   or spaghetti

2 egg whites

1 egg

1 green onion, thinly sliced

1 tablespoon dark sesame
   oil

4 ounces shiitake
   mushrooms, tough
   stems discarded, caps
   sliced *or* 1 package
   (4 ounces) sliced exotic
   mushrooms

2 cups thinly sliced bok
   choy (leaves and stems)

1 red or yellow bell pepper,
   cut into strips

½ cup vegetable broth

¼ cup teriyaki sauce

   Chopped peanuts
   (optional)

   Chopped fresh cilantro
   (optional)

1 Cook noodles according to package directions. Drain;
set aside.

2 Beat egg whites and egg in small bowl until foamy.
Stir in green onion. Spray large nonstick skillet with
nonstick cooking spray; heat over medium heat. Add
egg mixture; cook without stirring 2 to 3 minutes or until
bottom is set. Gently turn over; cook 1 minute or until
bottom is set. Slide onto cutting board; set aside.

3 Heat oil in same skillet over medium-high heat. Add
mushrooms, bok choy and bell pepper; cook 4 to
5 minutes or until vegetables are tender. Add broth and
teriyaki sauce; simmer 2 minutes. Remove to large bowl.
Add noodles; toss to coat.

4 Cut egg pancake into strips; add to noodle mixture.
Gently toss to combine. Serve with peanuts and cilantro,
if desired.

UDON NOODLES WITH CHICKEN AND SPINACH

MAKES 4 TO 6 SERVINGS

3 tablespoons vegetable oil, divided

4 boneless skinless chicken thighs (about 12 ounces), cut into bite-size pieces

2 teaspoons grated fresh ginger or ginger paste

2 cloves garlic, minced

1 cup chicken broth

6 cups (6 ounces) coarsely chopped baby spinach

2 green onions, chopped

1 package (8 ounces) udon noodles, cooked and drained

1 tablespoon soy sauce

1 Heat 2 tablespoons oil in large nonstick skillet over medium heat. Add chicken; cook and stir 4 to 6 minutes or until cooked through. Remove and drain on paper towels.

2 Heat remaining 1 tablespoon oil in skillet. Add ginger and garlic; cook over low heat 20 seconds or until garlic begins to brown. Add broth; bring to a simmer.

3 Stir in spinach and green onions. Cook 2 to 3 minutes or until spinach wilts. Stir in chicken and noodles. Season with soy sauce. Serve immediately.

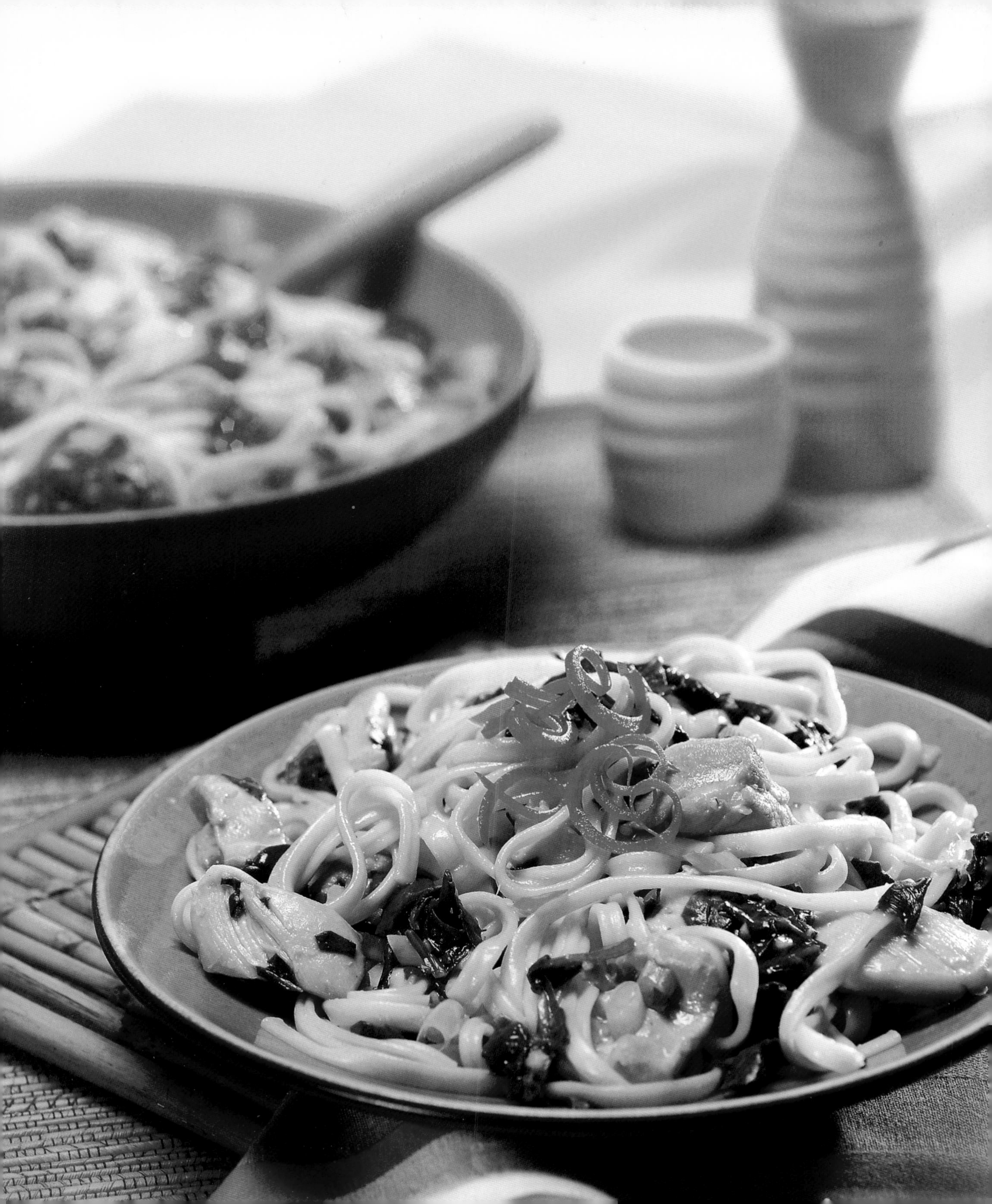

BANGKOK PEANUT NOODLES

MAKES 4 SERVINGS

SAUCE

- 6 tablespoons peanut butter
- ¼ cup soy sauce
- 1 tablespoon packed brown sugar
- 1 tablespoon rice vinegar
- 1 tablespoon sriracha sauce
- 2 teaspoons dark sesame oil
- 2 teaspoons grated fresh ginger or ginger paste
- 2 cloves garlic, minced

STIR-FRY

- 1 package (6 ounces) dried chow mein stir-fry noodles
- 1 pound boneless skinless chicken breasts, cut into 1-inch cubes *or* 1 package (14 ounces) extra firm tofu, cut into ½-inch cubes
- ½ cup cornstarch
- 3 tablespoons vegetable oil, divided
- 1 red bell pepper, cut into thin strips
- ½ medium onion, thinly sliced
- 2 cups sliced bok choy

  Lime wedges and chopped peanuts (optional)

1 For sauce, whisk peanut butter, soy sauce, brown sugar, vinegar, sriracha, sesame oil, ginger and garlic in medium bowl until smooth.

2 Cook noodles according to package directions; drain and rinse under cold water until cool.

3 Combine chicken and cornstarch in another medium bowl; toss to coat. Heat 2 tablespoons vegetable oil in large skillet over medium-high heat. Add chicken; stir-fry 5 minutes or until chicken is golden brown and cooked through. Drain on paper towel-lined plate. Wipe out skillet with paper towel.

4 Heat remaining 1 tablespoon vegetable oil in same skillet over high heat. Add bell pepper and onion; stir-fry 5 minutes or until browned. Add bok choy; stir-fry 1 minute or until wilted. Add noodles and sauce; cook until noodles are coated with sauce. Add 1 tablespoon water if needed to loosen sauce. Return chicken to skillet; stir to coat. Cook just until heated through. Serve immediately with lime wedges and peanuts, if desired.

SZECHUAN COLD NOODLES

MAKES 4 SERVINGS

8 ounces uncooked vermicelli, broken in half, or Chinese egg noodles

3 tablespoons rice vinegar

3 tablespoons soy sauce

2 tablespoons peanut or vegetable oil

1 clove garlic, minced

1 teaspoon minced fresh ginger or ginger paste

1 teaspoon dark sesame oil (optional)

½ teaspoon crushed Szechuan peppercorns or red pepper flakes

½ cup coarsely chopped fresh cilantro

¼ cup chopped peanuts

1 Cook vermicelli according to package directions; drain.

2 Combine vinegar, soy sauce, peanut oil, garlic, ginger, sesame oil, if desired, and peppercorns in large bowl. Add hot vermicelli; toss to coat. Sprinkle with cilantro and peanuts. Serve at room temperature or refrigerate until cold.

SZECHUAN VEGETABLE NOODLES: Add 1 cup chopped peeled cucumber, ½ cup *each* chopped red bell pepper and sliced green onions and an additional 1 tablespoon soy sauce.

SHRIMP AND NOODLES WITH CILANTRO PESTO

MAKES 2 TO 4 SERVINGS

½ cup plus 2 tablespoons chopped fresh cilantro, divided

1 jalapeño pepper, stemmed and seeded

2 tablespoons fresh lime juice

2 tablespoons rice vinegar or white vinegar

2 tablespoons water

2 tablespoons peanut butter

1½ tablespoons sugar

2 teaspoons soy sauce

¼ teaspoon red pepper flakes

4 ounces uncooked whole grain vermicelli or spaghetti, broken in half

8 ounces raw shrimp, peeled

3 ounces snow peas, cut in half diagonally

½ cup chopped green onions

2 ounces peanuts, toasted* and finely chopped

1 lime, quartered

To toast peanuts, spread in single layer in heavy skillet. Cook over medium heat 1 to 2 minutes or until nuts are lightly browned, stirring frequently.

1 For sauce, combine ½ cup cilantro, jalapeño, lime juice, vinegar, water, peanut butter, sugar, soy sauce and red pepper flakes in blender or food processor; blend until smooth.

2 Cook pasta according to package directions. Add shrimp during last 3 minutes of cooking; cook until shrimp are opaque and pasta is tender. Add snow peas; drain immediately. Transfer to large bowl.

3 Add sauce; stir until well blended. Sprinkle with green onions and peanuts; toss gently. Garnish with remaining 2 tablespoons cilantro and lime wedges.

SESAME NOODLES

MAKES 6 TO 8 SERVINGS

1 package (16 ounces) uncooked spaghetti

6 tablespoons soy sauce

5 tablespoons dark sesame oil

3 tablespoons sugar

3 tablespoons rice vinegar

2 tablespoons vegetable oil

3 cloves garlic, minced

1 teaspoon grated fresh ginger or ginger paste

½ teaspoon sriracha sauce

2 green onions, sliced

1 red bell pepper

1 cucumber

1 carrot

Sesame seeds (optional)

1 Cook spaghetti according to package directions until al dente in large saucepan of boiling salted water. Drain, reserving 1 tablespoon pasta cooking water.

2 Whisk soy sauce, sesame oil, sugar, vinegar, vegetable oil, garlic, ginger and sriracha in large bowl. Stir in noodles and green onions. Let stand at least 30 minutes until noodles have cooled to room temperature and most of sauce is absorbed, stirring occasionally.

3 Meanwhile, cut bell pepper into thin strips. Peel cucumber and carrot and shred with julienne peeler into long strands, or cut into thin strips. Stir into noodles. Serve at room temperature or refrigerate until ready to serve. Top with sesame seeds, if desired.

MEAT, CHICKEN & SEAFOOD

SPICY CHINESE PEPPER STEAK

MAKES 4 SERVINGS

1 boneless beef top sirloin steak (1 pound) or tenderloin tips, cut into thin strips

1 tablespoon cornstarch

3 cloves garlic, minced

½ teaspoon red pepper flakes

2 tablespoons peanut or canola oil, divided

1 green bell pepper, cut into thin strips

1 red bell pepper, cut into thin strips

¼ cup oyster sauce

2 tablespoons soy sauce

3 tablespoons chopped fresh cilantro or green onions

1 Combine beef, cornstarch, garlic and red pepper flakes in medium bowl; toss to coat.

2 Heat 1 tablespoon oil in wok or large skillet over medium-high heat. Add bell peppers; stir-fry 3 minutes. Transfer peppers to small bowl; set aside.

3 Heat remaining 1 tablespoon oil in wok. Add beef mixture; stir-fry 4 to 5 minutes or until beef is barely pink in center.

4 Add oyster sauce and soy sauce; stir-fry 1 minute. Return peppers to wok; stir-fry 1 to 2 minutes or until sauce thickens. Sprinkle with cilantro just before serving.

WALNUT CHICKEN

MAKES 4 SERVINGS

1 pound boneless skinless chicken thighs

3 tablespoons soy sauce

2 tablespoons minced fresh ginger or ginger paste

1 tablespoon cornstarch

1 tablespoon rice wine

2 cloves garlic, minced

¼ to ½ teaspoon red pepper flakes

3 tablespoons vegetable oil

½ cup walnut halves or pieces

1 cup frozen cut green beans, thawed or fresh green beans (1-inch pieces)

½ cup sliced water chestnuts

2 green onions, cut into 1-inch pieces

¼ cup water

Hot cooked rice

1 Cut chicken into 1-inch cubes. Combine soy sauce, ginger, cornstarch, wine, garlic and red pepper flakes in large bowl; stir until smooth. Add chicken; toss to coat. Marinate 10 minutes.

2 Heat wok or large skillet over high heat about 1 minute. Drizzle oil into wok and heat 30 seconds. Add walnuts; stir-fry about 1 minute or until lightly browned. Transfer to small bowl with slotted spoon.

3 Add chicken mixture to wok; stir-fry 5 to 7 minutes or until chicken is no longer pink in center. Add green beans, water chestnuts, green onions and water; stir-fry until heated through. Serve over rice. Sprinkle with walnuts.

SPICY PEANUT COCONUT SHRIMP

MAKES 4 SERVINGS

¼ cup shredded coconut

2 teaspoons dark sesame oil

1 pound large raw shrimp, peeled, deveined and patted dry

¼ to ½ teaspoon red pepper flakes

2 tablespoons chopped fresh mint or cilantro

¼ cup chopped salted roasted peanuts

Lime wedges (optional)

1 Heat large nonstick skillet over medium-high heat. Add coconut; cook and stir 2 to 3 minutes or until golden. Transfer to bowl.

2 Heat oil in same skillet over medium-high heat. Add shrimp and red pepper flakes; stir-fry 3 to 4 minutes or until shrimp are pink and opaque. Add mint; toss well and transfer to serving plates. Top each serving with 1 tablespoon toasted coconut and 1 tablespoon chopped peanuts. Garnish with lime wedges.

MANDARIN ORANGE CHICKEN

MAKES 6 SERVINGS

2 tablespoons rice vinegar

2 tablespoons olive oil, divided

2 tablespoons soy sauce

2 teaspoons grated orange peel

1 clove garlic, minced

1 pound boneless skinless chicken breasts, cut into strips

2 cans (11 ounces each) mandarin oranges, undrained

½ cup orange juice

2 tablespoons cornstarch

½ teaspoon red pepper flakes

1 onion, cut into thin wedges

1 small zucchini, thinly sliced

1 red bell pepper, cut into 1-inch pieces

Hot cooked rice

1 Whisk vinegar, 1 tablespoon oil, soy sauce, orange peel and garlic in medium bowl until well blended. Add chicken; toss to coat. Cover and marinate in refrigerator 15 minutes to 1 hour.

2 Drain chicken, reserving marinade. Drain oranges into 2-cup measuring cup; reserve oranges. Add marinade to cup, plus enough orange juice to measure 2 cups liquid, if necessary. Whisk orange juice mixture, cornstarch and red pepper flakes in medium bowl until smooth and well blended.

3 Heat remaining 1 tablespoon oil in wok or large skillet over high heat. Add chicken; stir-fry 2 to 3 minutes or until cooked through. Transfer to large bowl.

4 Add onion to wok; stir-fry 1 minute. Add zucchini; stir-fry 1 minute. Add bell pepper; stir-fry 1 minute or until all vegetables are crisp-tender.

5 Stir orange juice mixture until smooth; add to wok. Bring to a boil; boil 1 minute. Return chicken to wok; cook until heated through. Gently stir in oranges. Serve with rice.

TONKATSU (BREADED PORK CUTLETS)

MAKES 4 SERVINGS

TONKATSU SAUCE

¼ cup ketchup

1 tablespoon soy sauce

2 teaspoons sugar

2 teaspoons mirin
    (Japanese sweet rice
    wine)

1 teaspoon Worcestershire
    sauce

½ teaspoon grated fresh
    ginger or ginger paste

1 clove garlic, minced

PORK

1 pound pork tenderloin,
    trimmed of fat

½ cup all-purpose flour

2 eggs

2 tablespoons water

1½ cups panko bread crumbs

6 to 8 tablespoons
    vegetable oil, divided

   Salt and black pepper

   Hot cooked rice

1 For sauce, whisk ketchup, soy sauce, sugar, mirin, Worcestershire sauce, ginger and garlic in small bowl.

2 Slice pork diagonally into ½-inch-thick pieces. Spread flour on plate. Whisk eggs and 2 tablespoons water in shallow bowl. Spread panko on medium plate. Dip each pork slice first in flour, then egg mixture. Shake off excess and coat in panko.

3 Heat 2 tablespoons oil in large nonstick skillet over medium heat. Add pork in single layer without crowding. Cook 4 minutes per side or until cooked thorough. Drain on paper towels; keep warm. Repeat with remaining oil and pork.

4 Season pork with salt and pepper. Thinly slice and serve over rice with sauce.

TEPPANYAKI
MAKES 4 SERVINGS

⅓ cup tamari or soy sauce

2 tablespoons mirin (Japanese sweet rice wine)

1 tablespoon lemon juice

1 tablespoon orange juice

⅛ to ¼ teaspoon red pepper flakes (optional)

4 small frozen corn on the cob, thawed

2 to 3 tablespoons vegetable oil

2 zucchini or yellow squash, thinly sliced diagonally

4 ounces shiitake mushrooms, stemmed and cut into thick slices

8 ounces beef tenderloin or top loin steak, thinly sliced crosswise

8 ounces pork tenderloin, thinly sliced crosswise

8 ounces medium raw shrimp, peeled and deveined

1 For dipping sauce, combine tamari, mirin, lemon juice, orange juice and red pepper flakes, if desired, in small bowl; set aside.

2 Heat oven to 225°F to keep food warm while cooking. Cook corn in microwave according to package directions just until heated through. Heat large cast iron or other heavy skillet over medium-high heat. Brush with oil. Brown corn about 2 minutes, turning frequently. Transfer to large baking sheet in oven to keep warm.

3 Add zucchini to same skillet. Cook 2 to 3 minutes until browned and tender, adding oil if needed. Transfer to oven to keep warm. Cook mushrooms 2 to 3 minutes or until tender; keep warm in oven.

4 Cook beef 2 minutes or until browned and tender, adding more oil as needed; keep warm. Cook pork about 3 minutes or until cooked through; keep warm. Cook shrimp, stirring occasionally 2 to 3 minutes or until pink and opaque.

5 Arrange vegetables and meat on warm serving plates. Serve with dipping sauce.

SERVING SUGGESTION: Teppanyaki is often served with several dipping sauces. A traditional ponzu sauce, as in this recipe, is usually one of them. For a ginger dipping sauce, add minced fresh ginger, sake and a bit of wasabi to tamari or soy sauce.

THAI COCONUT CHICKEN MEATBALLS

MAKES 4 TO 5 SERVINGS

1 pound ground chicken

2 green onions, chopped

1 clove garlic, minced

2 teaspoons dark sesame oil

2 teaspoons mirin (Japanese rice wine)

1 teaspoon fish sauce

1 tablespoon canola oil

½ cup unsweetened canned coconut milk

¼ cup chicken broth

2 teaspoons packed brown sugar

1 teaspoon Thai red curry paste

2 teaspoons lime juice

2 tablespoons water

1 tablespoon cornstarch

SLOW COOKER DIRECTIONS

1 Combine chicken, green onions, garlic, sesame oil, mirin and fish sauce in large bowl. Shape into 1½-inch meatballs.

2 Heat canola oil in large skillet over medium-high heat. Working in batches, brown meatballs on all sides. Transfer to slow cooker. Add coconut milk, broth, brown sugar and curry paste. Cover; cook on HIGH 3½ to 4 hours. Stir in lime juice.

3 Stir water into cornstarch in small bowl until smooth. Stir into sauce in slow cooker. Cook, uncovered, on HIGH 10 to 15 minutes or until sauce is slightly thickened.

TIP: Meatballs that are of equal sizes will cook at the same rate and be done at the same time. To ensure your meatballs are the same size, pat seasoned ground meat into an even rectangle and then slice into even rows and columns. Roll each portion into a smooth ball.

KOREAN-STYLE SKIRT STEAK
MAKES 4 SERVINGS

1 pound skirt steak, cut into 4 pieces and pounded to ¼-inch thickness

½ cup sliced green onions

⅓ cup soy sauce

¼ cup unseasoned rice vinegar

2 tablespoons packed brown sugar

1 tablespoon dark sesame oil

1 clove garlic, minced

1 teaspoon grated fresh ginger or ginger paste

½ teaspoon red pepper flakes

Hot cooked noodles or rice

1 tablespoon toasted sesame seeds (optional)

1 Place steaks in large resealable food storage bag. Combine green onions, soy sauce, vinegar, brown sugar, oil, garlic, ginger and red pepper flakes in medium bowl. Reserve ⅓ cup marinade; pour remaining marinade over steak. Seal bag; turn to coat. Marinate in refrigerator 20 minutes or up to 4 hours.

2 Prepare grill for direct cooking.

3 Remove steaks from marinade; discard marinade. Grill steaks, covered, over medium heat 4 to 6 minutes or until medium rare, turning once.

4 Transfer steaks to cutting board; cover loosely with foil. Let stand 5 minutes before thinly slicing against the grain. Stir some of reserved marinade into noodles. Serve with beef and garnish with sesame seeds.

ASIAN CHICKEN FONDUE

MAKES 6 TO 8 SERVINGS

2 cups chicken broth

1 cup stemmed shiitake
   mushrooms

1 small leek, chopped

1 head baby bok choy,
   coarsely chopped

2 tablespoons oyster sauce

1 tablespoon mirin
   (Japanese rice wine)

1 tablespoon teriyaki sauce

2 pounds boneless skinless
   chicken breasts, cut into
   1-inch cubes

   Salt and black pepper

1 tablespoon canola oil

1 cup peeled cubed
   butternut squash

2 tablespoons cold water

1 tablespoon cornstarch

1 can (8 ounces) baby corn,
   drained

1 can (8 ounces) water
   chestnuts, drained

SLOW COOKER DIRECTIONS

1 Combine broth, mushrooms, leek, bok choy, oyster sauce, mirin and teriyaki sauce in slow cooker. Cover and turn slow cooker to LOW.

2 Season chicken with salt and pepper. Heat oil in large skillet over medium-high heat. Add chicken; cook without stirring 4 minutes or until browned on bottom. Turn and brown other side. Stir chicken and squash into slow cooker.

3 Cover; cook on LOW 4½ to 5 hours. Stir water into cornstarch in small bowl. Stir cornstarch mixture, baby corn and water chestnuts into slow cooker. Cover; cook on LOW 20 minutes or until baby corn is heated through. Serve with bamboo skewers, fondue forks or tongs.

THAI-STYLE PORK KABOBS

MAKES 4 SERVINGS

⅓ cup soy sauce

2 tablespoons fresh lime juice

2 tablespoons water

2 teaspoons hot chili oil*

2 cloves garlic, minced

1 teaspoon minced fresh ginger or ginger paste

12 ounces pork tenderloin, trimmed of fat

1 red or yellow bell pepper, cut into ½-inch pieces

1 red or sweet onion, cut into ½-inch chunks

2 cups hot cooked rice

* If hot chili oil is not available, combine 2 teaspoons vegetable oil and ½ teaspoon red pepper flakes in small microwavable bowl. Microwave on HIGH 30 to 45 seconds. Let stand 5 minutes to allow flavors to develop.

1 Whisk soy sauce, lime juice, water, chili oil, garlic and ginger in medium bowl until well blended. Reserve ⅓ cup for dipping sauce.

2 Cut pork into ½-inch strips. Add to remaining soy sauce mixture; toss to coat evenly. Cover and refrigerate at least 30 minutes or up to 2 hours, turning once.

3 Spray grid with nonstick cooking spray. Prepare grill for direct cooking.

4 Remove pork from marinade; discard marinade. Alternately thread pork strips, bell pepper and onion onto eight 8- to 10-inch skewers.**

5 Grill, covered, over medium heat 6 to 8 minutes or until pork is barely pink in center, turning once.

6 Serve with rice and reserved dipping sauce.

**If using bamboo skewers, soak in cold water 20 minutes to prevent burning.

HOT AND SOUR SHRIMP

MAKES 4 SERVINGS

½ (1-ounce) package dried shiitake or black Chinese mushrooms*

½ small cucumber

1 tablespoon packed brown sugar

2 teaspoons cornstarch

3 tablespoons rice vinegar

2 tablespoons soy sauce

1 tablespoon vegetable oil

1 pound medium raw shrimp, peeled and deveined

2 cloves garlic, minced

¼ teaspoon red pepper flakes

1 large red bell pepper, cut into short, thin strips

Hot cooked Chinese egg noodles or ramen noodles** (optional)

Or substitute ¾ cup sliced fresh mushrooms. Omit step 1.

**Discard seasoning packet.*

1 Place mushrooms in small bowl; cover with warm water. Soak 20 minutes to soften. Drain and squeeze out excess water. Discard stems; slice caps.

2 Cut cucumber in half lengthwise; scrape out seeds. Cut crosswise into ¼-inch slices.

3 Combine brown sugar and cornstarch in small bowl. Whisk in vinegar and soy sauce until smooth.

4 Heat oil in wok or large nonstick skillet over medium heat. Add shrimp, garlic and red pepper flakes; stir-fry 1 minute. Add mushrooms and bell pepper; stir-fry 2 minutes or until shrimp are pink and opaque.

5 Stir vinegar mixture; add to wok. Cook and stir 30 seconds or until sauce boils and thickens. Add cucumber; stir-fry until heated through. Serve over noodles, if desired.

TWICE-FRIED CHICKEN THIGHS WITH PLUM SAUCE

MAKES 4 SERVINGS

PLUM SAUCE

- 1 cup plum preserves
- ½ cup prepared chutney, chopped
- 2 tablespoons packed brown sugar
- 2 tablespoons lemon juice
- 2 cloves garlic, minced
- 2 teaspoons soy sauce
- 2 teaspoons minced fresh ginger or ginger paste

CHICKEN

- 1 cup peanut oil
- 1 to 1¼ pounds boneless skinless chicken thighs, cut into strips
- 4 carrots, julienned
- 4 green onions, sliced
- ½ teaspoon salt
- ½ teaspoon red pepper flakes

  Hot cooked rice
- 1 tablespoon sesame seeds, toasted*

To toast sesame seeds, spread in small skillet. Shake skillet over medium-low heat about 3 minutes or until seeds begin to pop and turn golden.

1. For plum sauce, combine plum preserves, chutney, brown sugar, lemon juice, garlic, soy sauce and ginger in small saucepan. Cook and stir over medium heat until preserves are melted and sauce is heated through.

2. Heat oil in wok over high heat to 375°F. Add chicken; fry 1 minute. Remove with slotted spoon; drain on paper towels. Drain oil from wok, reserving 2 tablespoons.

3. Heat 1 tablespoon reserved oil in wok over high heat. Add carrots; stir-fry 5 minutes until crisp-tender.

4. Add remaining 1 tablespoon oil to wok. Add chicken and green onions; stir-fry 1 minute. Stir in ½ cup plum sauce, salt and red pepper flakes. Stir-fry 2 minutes. Serve over rice; sprinkle with sesame seeds.

ORANGE BEEF

MAKES 4 SERVINGS

1 pound boneless beef top sirloin or tenderloin steaks

2 cloves garlic, minced

1 teaspoon grated orange peel

2 tablespoons soy sauce

2 tablespoons orange juice

1 tablespoon dry sherry

1 tablespoon cornstarch

1 tablespoon peanut or vegetable oil

Hot cooked rice (optional)

1 Cut beef in half lengthwise, then cut crosswise into thin slices. Toss with garlic and orange peel in medium bowl.

2 Blend soy sauce, orange juice and sherry into cornstarch in small bowl until smooth.

3 Heat oil in wok or large skillet over medium-high heat. Stir-fry beef in batches 2 to 3 minutes or until barely pink in center. Return all beef to wok.

4 Stir soy sauce mixture and add to wok. Cook and stir 30 seconds or until sauce boils and thickens. Serve over rice, if desired.

EASY MOO SHU PORK

MAKES 2 SERVINGS

1 tablespoon vegetable oil

8 ounces pork tenderloin, sliced

4 green onions, cut into ½-inch pieces

1½ cups packaged coleslaw mix

2 tablespoons hoisin sauce or Asian plum sauce

4 (8-inch) flour tortillas, warmed

1 Heat oil in large nonstick skillet over medium-high heat. Add pork and green onions; stir-fry 2 to 3 minutes or until pork is barely pink. Stir in coleslaw mix and hoisin sauce; stir-fry until heated through and cabbage is slightly wilted.

2 Spoon pork mixture onto tortillas. Fold bottom up and roll up tortillas to enclose filling.

NOTE: To warm tortillas, stack and wrap loosely in plastic wrap. Microwave on HIGH for 15 to 20 seconds or until hot and pliable.

THAI BARBECUED CHICKEN

MAKES 4 SERVINGS

1 cup coarsely chopped fresh cilantro

2 jalapeño peppers, stemmed and seeded

8 cloves garlic

2 tablespoons fish sauce

1 tablespoon packed brown sugar

1 teaspoon curry powder

Grated peel of 1 lemon

3 pounds bone-in chicken pieces

1 Combine cilantro, jalapeños, garlic, fish sauce, brown sugar, curry powder and lemon peel in food processor or blender; process until coarse paste forms.

2 Work fingers between skin and meat on breast and thigh pieces. Rub about 1 teaspoon seasoning paste under skin on each piece. Rub remaining paste all over chicken pieces. Place chicken in large resealable food storage bag or covered container; refrigerate 3 to 4 hours or overnight.

3 Prepare grill for direct cooking.

4 Grill chicken, covered, skin side down, over medium heat about 10 minutes or until well browned. Turn chicken and grill 20 to 30 minutes or until chicken is cooked through (165°F). Thighs and legs may require 5 to 10 minutes more cooking time than breasts. If chicken is browned on both sides but still needs additional cooking, move to edge of grill, away from direct heat, to finish cooking.

NOTE: To cook in oven, place chicken skin side up in lightly oiled baking pan. Bake in preheated 375°F oven 30 to 45 minutes or until chicken is cooked through (165°F).

CHINESE PEPPERCORN BEEF

MAKES 4 SERVINGS

2 teaspoons whole black and pink peppercorns*

2 teaspoons coriander seeds

1 tablespoon peanut or canola oil

1 boneless beef top sirloin steak, about 1¼ inches thick (1¼ to 1½ pounds)

2 teaspoons dark sesame oil

½ cup thinly sliced shallots or sweet onion

½ cup chicken broth

2 tablespoons soy sauce

1 tablespoon dry sherry

1 tablespoon cold water

1 teaspoon cornstarch

2 tablespoons thinly sliced green onion or chopped fresh cilantro

Or use all black peppercorns.

1 Place peppercorns and coriander seeds in small resealable food storage bag; seal bag. Coarsely crush spices using meat mallet or bottom of heavy saucepan. Brush peanut oil over both sides of steak; sprinkle with peppercorn mixture, pressing lightly.

2 Heat large heavy skillet over medium-high heat. Add steak; cook 4 minutes without moving or until seared on bottom. Reduce heat to medium; turn steak and continue cooking 3 to 4 minutes for medium-rare or until desired doneness. Transfer steak to cutting board; tent with foil and let stand while preparing sauce.

3 Add sesame oil to same skillet; heat over medium heat. Add shallots; cook and stir 3 minutes, stirring frequently. Add broth, soy sauce and sherry; simmer 2 minutes.

4 Stir water into cornstarch in small bowl; mix well. Add to skillet; cook and stir 3 to 4 minutes or until sauce thickens. Carve steak crosswise into thin slices. Spoon sauce over steak; sprinkle with green onion.

MOO GOO GAI PAN

MAKES 4 SERVINGS

1 package (1 ounce) dried shiitake mushrooms

¼ cup soy sauce

2 tablespoons rice vinegar

3 cloves garlic, minced

1 pound boneless skinless chicken breasts

½ cup chicken broth

1 tablespoon cornstarch

2 tablespoons peanut or vegetable oil, divided

1 can (about 7 ounces) straw mushrooms, rinsed and drained

3 green onions, cut into 1-inch pieces

Hot cooked noodles or rice (optional)

1 Place dried mushrooms in small bowl; cover with boiling water. Soak 20 minutes to soften. Drain; squeeze out excess water. Discard stems; slice caps.

2 Combine soy sauce, vinegar and garlic in medium bowl. Cut chicken crosswise into ½-inch strips. Add to soy sauce mixture; toss to coat. Marinate 20 minutes at room temperature. Blend broth into cornstarch in small bowl until smooth.

3 Heat 1 tablespoon oil in wok or large skillet over medium-high heat. Drain chicken, reserving marinade. Add chicken to wok; stir-fry 3 minutes or until cooked through. Transfer to plate; set aside.

4 Heat remaining 1 tablespoon oil in wok. Add dried mushrooms, straw mushrooms and green onions; stir-fry 1 minute.

5 Stir cornstarch mixture; add to wok with reserved marinade. Bring to a boil; boil 1 minute or until sauce thickens. Return chicken along with any accumulated juices to wok; cook and stir until heated through. Serve over noodles, if desired.

MISO SALMON
MAKES 4 SERVINGS

1 cup uncooked long grain rice

4 salmon fillets (about 6 ounces each)

¼ cup packed brown sugar

¼ cup red or white miso

2 tablespoons soy sauce

1 tablespoon hot water

1 tablespoon butter

1 tablespoon minced fresh ginger or ginger paste

1 tablespoon minced shallot or red onion

½ cup plus 1 teaspoon sake, divided

1 tablespoon whipping cream or half-and-half

½ cup (1 stick) cold butter, cut into small pieces

1 teaspoon lime juice

½ teaspoon salt

2 green onions, cut into julienne strips

1 Cook rice according to package directions; keep warm.

2 Preheat broiler. Spray 13×9-inch baking pan with nonstick cooking spray. Place salmon in prepared pan.

3 Whisk brown sugar, miso, soy sauce and hot water in small bowl until well blended. Spoon half of mixture evenly over fish. Broil 10 minutes or until fish begins to flake when tested with fork, spooning remaining mixture over fish twice during cooking.

4 Meanwhile, melt 1 tablespoon butter in small saucepan over medium heat. Add ginger and shallot; cook and stir 3 minutes or until softened. Add ½ cup sake; bring to a boil over medium-high heat. Cook 3 to 5 minutes or until reduced to 2 tablespoons.

5 Whisk in cream. Add cold butter, one piece at a time, whisking constantly until butter is incorporated before adding next piece. Remove from heat; whisk in remaining 1 teaspoon sake, lime juice and ½ teaspoon salt. Season with additional salt, if desired.

6 Spread sauce on 4 plates; top with rice, fish and green onions.

CARAMELIZED LEMONGRASS CHICKEN

MAKES 4 SERVINGS

2 stalks lemongrass

1½ pounds skinless chicken thighs (4 to 6 thighs)

3 tablespoons fish sauce

¼ cup sugar

2 cloves garlic, slivered

¼ teaspoon black pepper

1 tablespoon vegetable oil

1 tablespoon lemon juice

1 Remove outer leaves from lemongrass and discard. Trim off and discard upper stalks. Flatten lemongrass with meat mallet. Cut lemongrass into 1-inch pieces.

2 Place chicken in large resealable food storage bag; add fish sauce, sugar, garlic, pepper and lemongrass. Seal bag tightly; turn to coat. Marinate in refrigerator at least 1 hour or up to 4 hours, turning occasionally.

3 Heat oil in large skillet over medium heat. Remove chicken from bag; reserve marinade. Cook chicken 10 minutes or until browned, turning once.

4 Pour reserved marinade into skillet; bring to a boil. Boil 1 minute. Reduce heat to low; cover and simmer 30 minutes or until chicken is tender and no longer pink in center, turning chicken occasionally.

5 Stir lemon juice into skillet; turn chicken to coat.

INDIAN INSPIRED

KHEER

MAKES 6 TO 8 SERVINGS

4 cups whole milk

¾ cup sugar

1 cup uncooked white basmati rice, rinsed and drained

½ cup golden raisins

3 whole green cardamom pods *or* ¼ teaspoon ground cardamom

   Chopped pistachios

SLOW COOKER DIRECTIONS

1 Coat inside of slow cooker with nonstick cooking spray. Add milk and sugar; stir until sugar is dissolved. Add rice, raisins and cardamom.

2 Cover; cook on HIGH 1 hour. Stir. Cover; cook on HIGH 1½ to 2 hours or until milk is absorbed. Serve warm or cold. Garnish with pistachios.

CHAPATIS

MAKES 16 CHAPATIS

2 cups whole wheat flour
(or a combination of
whole wheat and
all-purpose flour)

1 tablespoon vegetable oil

1 teaspoon salt

¾ to 1 cup warm water

1 Combine flour, oil and salt in bowl of food processor. With motor running, slowly drizzle ¾ cup water through feed tube; process until dough forms a ball that cleans the sides of the bowl. Let stand 2 minutes.

2 Turn on processor and slowly add more water until dough is soft but not sticky. If dough is hard or dry, cut it into quarters and sprinkle water over the quarters. Process until dough forms soft ball, gradually adding more water if dough will absorb it. Let dough stand in work bowl 5 minutes.

3 Turn dough onto lightly greased surface and shape into a ball. Cover with inverted bowl or plastic wrap and let stand at room temperature 1 hour.

4 Uncover dough; divide into 16 equal pieces. Roll out each piece on lightly floured surface to a thin circle 6 to 8 inches in diameter.

5 Heat an ungreased electric griddle to 375°F, or heat a large ungreased skillet over medium heat until hot enough to sizzle a drop of water. Cook each chapati until golden, about 1 minute on each side, pressing with wide spatula to cook evenly. Serve hot.

CHICKEN TIKKA MASALA MEATBALLS

MAKES 6 SERVINGS

MEATBALLS

- 1 pound ground chicken
- ½ cup plain dry bread crumbs
- ¼ cup finely chopped onion
- 1 egg
- 2 tablespoons chopped fresh cilantro
- 1 tablespoon minced fresh ginger or ginger paste
- 1 tablespoon tomato paste
- 2 cloves garlic, minced
- ½ teaspoon salt

TIKKA MASALA SAUCE

- 2 teaspoons sugar
- 2 teaspoons ground coriander
- 1 teaspoon ground cumin
- ½ teaspoon salt
- ½ teaspoon ground mustard seed
- ½ teaspoon ground red pepper
- 1 tablespoon vegetable oil
- ½ cup finely chopped onion
- 2 tablespoons minced fresh ginger or ginger paste
- 3 cloves garlic, minced
- 1 medium tomato, finely diced
- ½ cup water
- ½ cup canned coconut milk
- 1 tablespoon tomato paste
- ¼ cup chopped fresh cilantro

1 Preheat oven to 400°F. Line rimmed baking sheet with parchment paper.

2 Combine chicken, bread crumbs, ¼ cup onion, egg, 2 tablespoons cilantro, 1 tablespoon ginger, 1 tablespoon tomato paste, 2 cloves garlic and ½ teaspoon salt in large bowl; mix well. Shape into 30 tablespoon-size meatballs. Place on prepared baking sheet. Bake 20 minutes.

3 Meanwhile for sauce, combine sugar, coriander, cumin, ½ teaspoon salt, mustard and red pepper in small bowl.

4 Heat oil in medium saucepan over medium heat. Add ½ cup onion; cook and stir 5 minutes or until just beginning to brown. Add 2 tablespoons ginger, spice mixture and 3 cloves garlic; cook and stir 1 minute. Add tomato, water, coconut milk and 1 tablespoon tomato paste. Reduce heat to low; cook 10 minutes to allow flavors to develop. Add meatballs to saucepan; gently stir to coat evenly.

5 Spoon meatballs onto serving plates. Sprinkle with ¼ cup cilantro.

SERVING SUGGESTION: Serve with whole wheat naan bread or over hot cooked brown rice.

INDIAN-STYLE LAMB AND CHICKPEAS

MAKES 6 TO 8 SERVINGS

2 tablespoons butter, divided

1 onion, chopped

3 cloves garlic, chopped

2 teaspoons finely chopped fresh ginger or ginger paste

1 pound ground lamb

Salt and black pepper

1 pound (about 3 medium) fresh tomatoes, diced

1 tablespoon curry powder

½ teaspoon ground red pepper

⅛ teaspoon ground cinnamon

⅛ teaspoon ground nutmeg

2 cans (about 15 ounces each) chickpeas, rinsed and drained

¾ cup plain full-fat yogurt

½ cup plain dry bread crumbs

1 Preheat oven to 350°F. Melt 1 tablespoon butter in large skillet over medium-high heat. Add onion, garlic and ginger; cook and stir 2 minutes or until onion begins to soften. Add lamb; cook until no longer pink, stirring to break up meat. Season with salt and black pepper.

2 Add tomatoes, curry powder, red pepper, cinnamon and nutmeg; cook and stir 5 minutes. Remove from heat. Add chickpeas and yogurt; stir to combine.

3 Transfer mixture to 2- to 2½-quart casserole. Sprinkle bread crumbs on top and dot with remaining 1 tablespoon butter. Bake 30 minutes or until bubbly and lightly browned.

PAKORAS

MAKES 4 TO 6 SERVINGS

Tamarind Sauce
(recipe follows)

1½ cups chickpea flour

2 teaspoons salt

1 teaspoon baking soda

½ teaspoon ground turmeric

½ teaspoon chili powder

¼ teaspoon garlic powder

½ cup water

¼ cup plain yogurt

1 large zucchini, sliced into ¼-inch rounds

1 medium sweet potato, sliced into ¼-inch rounds

½ small butternut squash, peeled, seeded and sliced into ¼-inch-thick pieces

1 small Asian eggplant, sliced into ¼-inch rounds

4 cups canola oil

1 Prepare tamarind sauce.

2 Whisk flour, salt, baking soda, turmeric, chili powder and garlic powder in large bowl until well blended. Whisk water and yogurt in small bowl until well blended. Add enough yogurt mixture to flour mixture to make thick batter (similar to pancake batter).

3 Place vegetable slices in microwavable bowl with ¼ cup water. Cover with plastic wrap. Microwave on HIGH 2 minutes. Drain; cool slightly. Pat dry with paper towels.

4 Heat oil in deep saucepan until to 350°F.

5 Dip vegetable slices into batter; coat well. Carefully place vegetables in oil. Fry until golden brown, about 30 seconds per side. Drain on paper towels. Serve with tamarind sauce.

TAMARIND SAUCE: Combine 2 cups water, ⅓ cup sugar and 2 tablespoons tamarind paste in small saucepan. Bring to a boil over high heat. Reduce heat to low; simmer until mixture is reduced by two thirds. Cool before using.

INDIAN-STYLE APRICOT CHICKEN

MAKES 4 TO 6 SERVINGS

6 chicken thighs

¼ teaspoon salt

¼ teaspoon black pepper

1 tablespoon vegetable oil

1 large onion, chopped

2 tablespoons grated fresh
   ginger or ginger paste

2 cloves garlic, minced

½ teaspoon ground
   cinnamon

⅛ teaspoon ground allspice

1 can (about 14 ounces)
   diced tomatoes

1 cup chicken broth

1 package (8 ounces) dried
   apricots

1 pinch saffron (optional)

   Hot basmati rice

2 tablespoons chopped
   fresh parsley (optional)

SLOW COOKER DIRECTIONS

1 Coat slow cooker with nonstick cooking spray. Season
chicken with salt and pepper. Heat oil in large skillet over
medium-high heat. Brown chicken on all sides. Transfer
to slow cooker.

2 Add onion to skillet; cook and stir 5 minutes or until
translucent. Stir in ginger, garlic, cinnamon and allspice;
cook and stir 15 to 30 seconds or until fragrant. Add
tomatoes and broth; cook 2 to 3 minutes or until heated
through. Pour into slow cooker.

3 Add apricots and saffron, if desired. Cover; cook on
LOW 5 to 6 hours or on HIGH 3 to 3½ hours or until
chicken is tender. Serve with rice; garnish with parsley.

CHANNA CHAT (INDIAN-SPICED SNACK MIX)

MAKES 6 TO 8 SERVINGS

2 teaspoons canola oil

1 medium onion, finely chopped, divided

2 cloves garlic, minced

2 cans (about 15 ounces each) chickpeas, rinsed and drained

¼ cup vegetable broth or water

2 teaspoons tomato paste

¼ teaspoon ground cinnamon

¼ teaspoon ground cumin

¼ teaspoon black pepper

1 bay leaf

½ cup balsamic vinegar

1 tablespoon packed brown sugar

1 plum tomato, chopped

½ jalapeño pepper, minced *or* ¼ teaspoon ground red pepper (optional)

½ cup crisp rice cereal

3 tablespoons chopped fresh cilantro (optional)

SLOW COOKER DIRECTIONS

1 Heat oil in small skillet over medium heat. Add half of onion and garlic; cook and stir 2 minutes or until softened. Transfer to slow cooker. Stir chickpeas, broth, tomato paste, cinnamon, cumin, black pepper and bay leaf into slow cooker.

2 Cover; cook on LOW 6 hours or on HIGH 3 hours. Remove and discard bay leaf.

3 Transfer chickpeas to large shallow bowl with slotted spoon; let cool 15 minutes. Meanwhile, combine balsamic vinegar and brown sugar in small saucepan. Cook over medium-low heat until mixture becomes syrupy.

4 Toss chickpeas with tomato, remaining onion and jalapeño, if desired. Fold in rice cereal and drizzle with balsamic syrup. Garnish with cilantro.

CHICKPEA TIKKA MASALA

MAKES 4 SERVINGS

1 tablespoon olive oil

1 onion, chopped

3 cloves garlic, minced

1 tablespoon minced fresh ginger or ginger paste

1 tablespoon garam masala

1 teaspoon ground cumin

1 teaspoon ground coriander

1 teaspoon salt

¼ teaspoon ground red pepper

2 cans (15 ounces each) chickpeas, drained

1 can (28 ounces) crushed tomatoes

1 can (about 13 ounces) coconut milk

1 package (about 12 ounces) firm silken tofu, drained and cut into 1-inch cubes or paneer

Hot cooked brown basmati rice

Chopped fresh cilantro

1 Heat oil in large saucepan over medium-high heat. Add onion; cook and stir 5 minutes or until translucent. Add garlic, ginger, garam masala, cumin, coriander, salt and red pepper; cook and stir 1 minute.

2 Stir in chickpeas, tomatoes and coconut milk; simmer 30 minutes or until thickened and chickpeas have softened slightly. Add tofu; stir gently. Cook 7 to 10 minutes or until tofu is heated through. Serve over rice; garnish with cilantro.

KOFTAS (LAMB MEATBALLS IN SPICY GRAVY)

MAKES 6 SERVINGS

1½ pounds ground lamb or ground beef

1½ cups finely chopped onions, divided

2 eggs

½ cup chopped fresh cilantro

2 cloves garlic, minced

2 teaspoons garam masala

1 teaspoon minced fresh ginger

1½ teaspoons salt, divided

24 whole blanched almonds

1 tablespoon peanut oil

1 teaspoon ground coriander

1 teaspoon ground cumin

1 teaspoon chili powder

½ teaspoon ground turmeric

2 tomatoes, peeled, seeded and chopped

½ cup water

3 cups hot cooked basmati rice

1 cup plain yogurt

1 Combine lamb, ½ cup onion, eggs, cilantro, garlic, garam masala, ginger and ½ teaspoon salt in medium bowl; mix well. Refrigerate at least 1 hour or overnight.

2 Shape mixture into 24 ovals or balls; insert 1 almond into each meatball. Heat oil in large skillet over medium-high heat. Add half of meatballs; cook 8 minutes or until browned, turning frequently. Repeat with remaining meatballs. Transfer to plate.

3 Reduce heat to medium. Add remaining 1 cup onion; cook and stir 6 to 8 minutes or until browned. Stir in remaining 1 teaspoon salt, coriander, cumin, chili powder and turmeric. Add tomatoes; cook 5 minutes or until tomatoes are tender.

4 Add water; bring mixture to a boil over high heat. Add meatballs. Reduce heat to medium-low. Simmer 15 minutes or until cooked through. Place rice in serving bowls; top with meatballs.

5 Remove skillet from heat. Place yogurt in medium bowl; stir in several spoonfuls hot mixture. Stir yogurt mixture into sauce in skillet. Cook over medium-low heat until sauce thickens. Do not boil. Pour sauce over meatballs.

ONION BHAJI WITH CUCUMBER SAUCE

MAKES 10 FRITTERS AND 1¼ CUPS SAUCE

8 ounces seedless cucumber (about 8 inches)

½ cup plain Greek yogurt

1 clove garlic, minced

2 teaspoons chopped fresh mint

1 teaspoon salt, divided

2 yellow onions (8 ounces each)

½ cup chickpea flour

½ teaspoon baking powder

¼ teaspoon ground cumin

1 tablespoon minced fresh cilantro

¼ cup water

½ cup vegetable oil

1 For sauce, grate cucumber on large holes of box grater. Squeeze out excess liquid. Combine yogurt, garlic, mint and ½ teaspoon salt in medium bowl. Stir in cucumber. Refrigerate until ready to use.

2 For bhaji, cut onions in half and thinly slice. Whisk chickpea flour, baking powder, remaining ½ teaspoon salt and cumin in large bowl. Stir in cilantro. Whisk in water in thin steady stream until batter is the consistency of heavy cream. Add additional water by teaspoons if batter is too thick. Stir in onions until coated with batter.

3 Heat oil in large cast iron skillet over medium-high heat. Working in batches, drop level ¼ cupfuls of onion mixture into hot oil. Cook about 2 minutes or until bottoms are well browned. Turn and press lightly with spatula. Cook 2 minutes or until well browned on both sides. Drain on paper towels. Serve hot with cucumber sauce.

INDIAN-INSPIRED CHICKEN WITH RAITA

MAKES 6 TO 8 SERVINGS

1 cup plain yogurt

2 cloves garlic, minced

1 teaspoon salt

1 teaspoon ground coriander

1 teaspoon ground ginger

½ teaspoon ground turmeric

½ teaspoon ground cinnamon

½ teaspoon ground cumin

¼ teaspoon ground red pepper

1 (5- to 6-pound) chicken, cut into 8 pieces (about 4 pounds chicken parts)

1 Mix 1 cup yogurt, 2 cloves garlic, 1 teaspoon salt, coriander, ginger, turmeric, cinnamon, cumin and red pepper in medium bowl. Place chicken in large resealable food storage bag. Add yogurt mixture; marinate in refrigerator 4 to 24 hours, turning occasionally.

2 Preheat broiler. Cover baking sheet with foil. Place chicken on prepared baking sheet. Broil 6 inches from heat about 30 minutes or until cooked through (165°F), turning once.

3 Meanwhile, prepare raita. Serve with chicken.

RAITA: Peel 2 medium cucumbers and cut in half lengthwise. Scoop out seeds with spoon. Cut halves in half lengthwise and thinly slice. Place in medium bowl. Add ⅓ cup plain yogurt, 2 tablespoons chopped fresh cilantro or mint, 1 minced clove garlic, ¼ teaspoon salt and ⅛ teaspoon black pepper in small bowl. Serve with chicken.

CURRIED CAULIFLOWER AND POTATOES

MAKES 6 SERVINGS

3 tablespoons vegetable oil

1 medium onion, chopped

1 tablespoon minced garlic

1 tablespoon curry powder

1½ teaspoons salt

1½ teaspoons grated fresh
   ginger or garlic paste

1 teaspoon ground turmeric

1 teaspoon brown or yellow
   mustard seeds

¼ teaspoon red pepper flakes

1 medium head cauliflower,
   cut into 1-inch pieces

2 pounds fingerling potatoes,
   cut into halves

½ cup water

SLOW COOKER DIRECTIONS

1 Heat oil in medium skillet over medium heat. Add onion; cook 8 minutes or until softened. Add garlic, curry powder, salt, ginger, turmeric, mustard seeds and red pepper flakes; cook and stir 1 minute. Transfer onion mixture to slow cooker.

2 Stir in cauliflower, potatoes and water. Cover; cook on HIGH 4 hours.

A

Almond Milk Tea with Tapioca, 32
Asian Chicken Fondue, 142
Asian Fish Stew, 56
Asian Lettuce Wraps, 8
Asparagus
  Buddha's Delight, 94
  Chicken Stir-Fry with Cabbage Pancake, 82
Avocado: California Roll Farro Sushi Bowl, 100

B

Bangkok Peanut Noodles, 118
Bean Threads with Minced Pork, 92
Beef
  Chinese Peppercorn Beef, 156
  Five-Spice Beef and Bok Choy, 74
  Korean-Style Skirt Steak, 140
  Mini Marinated Beef Skewers, 28
  Orange Beef, 150
  Satay Beef, 12
  Sesame Beef with Pineapple-Plum Sauce, 90
  Spicy Chinese Pepper Steak, 127
  Teppanyaki, 136
Bell Peppers
  Asian Lettuce Wraps, 8
  Bangkok Peanut Noodles, 118
  Cashew Chicken, 78
  Chinese Crab and Cucumber Salad, 58
  Hot and Sour Shrimp, 146
  Mandarin Orange Chicken, 132
  Peanut Noodles, 111
  Sesame Beef with Pineapple-Plum Sauce, 90
  Sesame Noodles, 124Spiced Orange Chicken Kabob Appetizers, 14
  Spicy Chinese Pepper Steak, 127

Bell Peppers (continued)
  Szechuan Vegetable Noodles, 120
  Thai Basil Pork Stir-Fry, 76
  Thai Coconut Chicken and Rice Soup, 52
  Thai-Style Pork Kabobs, 144
  Tofu Satay Bowl, 108
  Vegetable Lo Mein, 114
Beverages
  Almond Milk Tea with Tapioca, 32
  Green Tea Lychee Frappé, 36
  Melon Bubble Tea, 34
Bok Choy
  Asian Chicken Fondue, 142
  Asian Fish Stew, 56
  Bangkok Peanut Noodles, 118
  Braised Cabbage, 60
  Five-Spice Beef and Bok Choy, 74
  Vegetable Lo Mein, 114
Braised Cabbage, 60
Broccoli
  Asian Fish Stew, 56
  Thai Basil Pork Stir-Fry, 76
  Thai Green Curry, 84
Buddha's Delight, 94
Butternut Squash in Coconut Milk, 39

C

Cabbage
  Asian Fish Stew, 56
  Asian Lettuce Wraps, 8
  Braised Cabbage, 60
  Chicken Stir-Fry with Cabbage Pancake, 82
  Easy Moo Shu Pork, 152
  Fukien Red-Cooked Pork, 70Ginger Chicken Pot Stickers, 16
  Lobster Pot Stickers, 22
  Mandarin Chicken Salad, 50
  Mini Egg Rolls, 5

Cabbage (continued)
  Orange-Ginger Ramen Slaw, 42
  Quick Chicken and Cabbage Sesame Noodles, 112
California Roll Farro Sushi Bowl, 100
Caramelized Lemongrass Chicken, 162
Cashew Chicken, 78
Cashew Green Beans, 66
Cauliflower: Curried Cauliflower and Potatoes, 186
Channa Chat (Indian-Spiced Snack Mix), 176
Chapatis, 166
Chicken
  Asian Chicken Fondue, 142
  Asian Lettuce Wraps, 8
  Bangkok Peanut Noodles, 118
  Caramelized Lemongrass Chicken, 162
  Cashew Chicken, 78
  Chicken Chow Mein, 69
  Chicken Congee, 99
  Chicken Fried Rice, 96
  Chicken Ramen Noodle Bowls, 106
  Chicken Stir-Fry with Cabbage Pancake, 82
  Chicken Tikka Masala Meatballs, 168
  Ginger Chicken Pot Stickers, 16
  Indian-Inspired Chicken with Raita, 184
  Indian-Style Apricot Chicken, 174
  Japanese Egg Drop Soup, 64
  Mandarin Chicken Salad, 50
  Mandarin Orange Chicken, 132
  Moo Goo Gai Pan, 158
  Pineapple Basil Chicken Supreme, 88
  Quick Chicken and Cabbage Sesame Noodles, 112
  Spiced Orange Chicken Kabob Appetizers, 14

Chicken (*continued*)
  Spicy Chicken Bundles, 26
  Spicy Thai Coconut Soup, 48
  Sweet and Spicy Chicken
    Wings, 6
  Sweet-Hot Orange Chicken
    Drumettes, 20
  Thai Barbecued Chicken, 154
  Thai Coconut Chicken and
    Rice Soup, 52
  Thai Coconut Chicken
    Meatballs, 138
  Three-Topped Rice, 104
  Twice-Fried Chicken Thighs
    with Plum Sauce, 148
  Udon Noodles with Chicken
    and Spinach, 116
  Walnut Chicken, 128
  Chicken Chow Mein, 69
  Chicken Congee, 99
  Chicken Fried Rice, 96
  Chicken Ramen Noodle Bowls,
    106
  Chicken Stir-Fry with Cabbage
    Pancake, 82
  Chicken Tikka Masala Meatballs,
    168
  Chickpea Tikka Masala, 178
Chickpeas
  Channa Chat (Indian-Spiced
    Snack Mix), 176
  Chickpea Tikka Masala, 178
  Indian-Style Lamb and
    Chickpeas, 170
  Chinese Crab and Cucumber
    Salad, 58
  Chinese Crab Cakes, 18
  Chinese Peppercorn Beef, 156
Coconut and Coconut Milk
  Butternut Squash in Coconut
    Milk, 39
  Chicken Tikka Masala
    Meatballs, 168
  Chickpea Tikka Masala, 178
  Melon Bubble Tea, 34
  Spicy Peanut Coconut Shrimp,
    130
  Spicy Thai Coconut Soup, 48

Coconut and Coconut Milk
  (*continued*)
  Thai Coconut Chicken and
    Rice Soup, 52
  Thai Coconut Chicken
    Meatballs, 138
  Thai Curried Vegetables, 62
  Thai Red Curry with Tofu, 102
  Tofu Satay Bowl, 108
Crab
  Chinese Crab and Cucumber
    Salad, 58
  Chinese Crab Cakes, 18
  Cucumber Relish, 108
Cucumbers
  California Roll Farro Sushi
    Bowl, 100
  Chinese Crab and Cucumber
    Salad, 58
  Cucumber Relish, 108
  Hot and Sour Shrimp, 146
  Indian-Inspired Chicken with
    Raita, 184
  Onion Bhaji with Cucumber
    Sauce, 182
  Sesame Noodles, 124
  Szechuan Vegetable Noodles,
    120
  Tofu Satay Bowl, 108
  Curried Cauliflower and
    Potatoes, 186
Curry, Thai Red
  Spicy Thai Coconut Soup, 48
  Thai Curried Vegetables, 62
  Thai Red Curry with Tofu, 102

E
Easy Moo Shu Pork, 152
Edamame
  Peanut Noodles, 111
  Wasabi Roasted Edamame, 10
Eggplant
  Pakoras, 172
  Thai Red Curry with Tofu, 102
Eggs
  Chicken Fried Rice, 96
  Chicken Stir-Fry with Cabbage
    Pancake, 82

Eggs (*continued*)
  Hot and Sour Soup, 40
  Japanese Egg Drop Soup,
    64
  Simple Fried Rice, 72
  Three-Topped Rice, 104
  Vegetable Lo Mein, 114

F
Farro: California Roll Farro Sushi
    Bowl, 100
Fish (*see also* **Crab; Shrimp;
    Surimi**)
  Asian Fish Stew, 56
  Miso Salmon, 160
  Five-Spice Beef and Bok Choy,
    74
  Fried Tofu with Asian
    Vegetables, 80
  Fukien Red-Cooked Pork, 70

G
Ginger Wonton Soup, 44
Ginger Chicken Pot Stickers, 16
Green Beans
  Cashew Green Beans, 66
  Spicy Green Beans, 46
  Thai Red Curry with Tofu,
    102
  Walnut Chicken, 128
Green Tea Lychee Frappé, 36

H
Hot and Sour Shrimp, 146
Hot and Sour Soup, 40

I
Indian-Inspired Chicken with
    Raita, 184
Indian-Style Apricot Chicken,
    174
Indian-Style Lamb and
    Chickpeas, 170

J
Japanese Egg Drop Soup, 64

K

Kheer, 165
Koftas (Lamb Meatballs in Spicy Gravy), 180
Korean-Style Skirt Steak, 140

L

Lamb
Indian-Style Lamb and Chickpeas, 170
Koftas (Lamb Meatballs in Spicy Gravy), 180
Lobster Pot Stickers, 22

M

Mandarin Chicken Salad, 50
Mandarin Orange Chicken, 132
Melon Bubble Tea, 34
Mini Egg Rolls, 5
Mini Marinated Beef Skewers, 28
Miso Salmon, 160
Moo Goo Gai Pan, 158
Mushrooms
Asian Chicken Fondue, 142
Asian Fish Stew, 56
Asian Lettuce Wraps, 8
Bean Threads with Minced Pork, 92
Buddha's Delight, 94
Cashew Chicken, 78
Chicken Ramen Noodle Bowls, 106
Chicken Stir-Fry with Cabbage Pancake, 82
Hot and Sour Shrimp, 146
Hot and Sour Soup, 40
Lobster Pot Stickers, 22
Moo Goo Gai Pan, 158
Portobello Mushrooms Sesame, 54
Spiced Orange Chicken Kabob Appetizers, 14
Spicy Thai Coconut Soup, 48
Teppanyaki, 136
Thai Coconut Chicken and Rice Soup, 52
Tofu Satay Bowl, 108

Mushrooms (continued)
Vegetable Lo Mein, 114
Vermicelli with Pork, 86

N

Noodles
Bangkok Peanut Noodles, 118
Bean Threads with Minced Pork, 92
Chicken Chow Mein, 69
Chicken Ramen Noodle Bowls, 106
Mandarin Chicken Salad, 50
Orange-Ginger Ramen Slaw, 42
Peanut Noodles, 111
Quick Chicken and Cabbage Sesame Noodles, 112
Sesame Noodles, 124
Shrimp Pad Thai, 122
Szechuan Cold Noodles, 120
Szechuan Vegetable Noodles, 120
Udon Noodles with Chicken and Spinach, 116
Vegetable Lo Mein, 114
Vermicelli with Pork, 86
Nuts (see also **Peanuts**)
Cashew Chicken, 78
Cashew Green Beans, 66
Koftas (Lamb Meatballs in Spicy Gravy), 180
Pineapple Basil Chicken Supreme, 88
Walnut Chicken, 128

O

Onion Bhaji with Cucumber Sauce, 182
Orange
Mandarin Chicken Salad, 50
Mandarin Orange Chicken, 132
Melon Bubble Tea, 34
Orange Beef, 150
Orange-Ginger Ramen Slaw, 42
Spiced Orange Chicken Kabob Appetizers, 14
Sweet-Hot Orange Chicken Drumettes, 20

Orange Beef, 150
Orange-Ginger Ramen Slaw, 42

P

Pakoras, 172
Peanut Butter
Bangkok Peanut Noodles, 118
Peanut Noodles, 111
Shrimp and Noodles with Cilantro Pesto, 122
Tofu Satay Bowl, 108
Peanut Noodles, 111
Peanuts
Asian Lettuce Wraps, 8
Quick Chicken and Cabbage Sesame Noodles, 112
Shrimp and Noodles with Cilantro Pesto, 122
Spicy Chicken Bundles, 26
Spicy Peanut Coconut Shrimp, 130
Szechuan Cold Noodles, 120
Szechuan Vegetable Noodles, 120
Pineapple
Pineapple Basil Chicken Supreme, 88
Sesame Beef with Pineapple-Plum Sauce, 90
Pineapple Basil Chicken Supreme, 88
Pork
Bean Threads with Minced Pork, 92
Easy Moo Shu Pork, 152
Fukien Red-Cooked Pork, 70
Ginger Wonton Soup, 44
Mini Egg Rolls, 5
Teppanyaki, 136
Thai Basil Pork Stir-Fry, 76
Thai-Style Pork Kabobs, 144
Tonkatsu (Breaded Pork Cutlets), 134
Vermicelli with Pork, 86
Portobello Mushrooms Sesame, 54
Potatoes: Curried Cauliflower and Potatoes, 186

Potatoes, Sweet
Pakoras, 172
Thai Red Curry with Tofu, 102

Q

Quick Chicken and Cabbage
Sesame Noodles, 112

R

Rice
Chicken Congee, 99
Chicken Fried Rice, 96
Kheer, 165
Koftas (Lamb Meatballs in
Spicy Gravy), 180
Miso Salmon, 160
Simple Fried Rice, 72
Thai Coconut Chicken and
Rice Soup, 52
Three-Topped Rice, 104

S

Salads
Chinese Crab and Cucumber
Salad, 58
Mandarin Chicken Salad, 50
Orange-Ginger Ramen Slaw,
42
Satay Beef, 12
Scallion Pancakes, 30
Sesame Beef with Pineapple-
Plum Sauce, 90
Sesame Noodles, 124
Shrimp
Asian Fish Stew, 56
Asian Lettuce Wraps, 8
Hot and Sour Shrimp, 146
Shrimp and Noodles with
Cilantro Pesto, 122
Simple Fried Rice, 72
Spicy Crispy Shrimp, 24
Spicy Peanut Coconut Shrimp,
130
Teppanyaki, 136
Shrimp and Noodles with
Cilantro Pesto, 122
Simple Fried Rice, 72

Slow Cooker Recipes
Asian Chicken Fondue, 142
Asian Lettuce Wraps, 8
Channa Chat (Indian-Spiced
Snack Mix), 176
Chicken Congee, 99
Chicken Ramen Noodle Bowls,
106
Curried Cauliflower and
Potatoes, 186
Indian-Style Apricot Chicken,
174
Kheer, 165
Thai Coconut Chicken and
Rice Soup, 52
Thai Coconut Chicken
Meatballs, 138
Thai Red Curry with Tofu, 102
Spiced Orange Chicken Kabob
Appetizers, 14
Spicy Green Beans, 46
Spicy Chicken Bundles, 26
Spicy Chinese Pepper Steak, 127
Spicy Crispy Shrimp, 24
Spicy Peanut Coconut Shrimp,
130
Spicy Thai Coconut Soup, 48
Soups
Asian Fish Stew, 56
Ginger Wonton Soup, 44
Hot and Sour Soup, 40
Japanese Egg Drop Soup, 64
Spicy Thai Coconut Soup, 48
Thai Coconut Chicken and
Rice Soup, 52
Squash, Butternut
Asian Chicken Fondue, 142
Butternut Squash in Coconut
Milk, 39
Pakoras, 172
Surimi
California Roll Farro Sushi
Bowl, 100
Lobster Pot Stickers, 22
Sweet and Spicy Chicken Wings,
6
Sweet-Hot Orange Chicken
Drumettes, 20
Szechuan Cold Noodles, 120
Szechuan Vegetable Noodles, 120

T

Tamarind Sauce, 172
Teppanyaki, 136
Thai Barbecued Chicken, 154
Thai Basil Pork Stir-fry, 76
Thai Coconut Chicken and Rice
Soup, 52
Thai Coconut Chicken Meatballs,
138
Thai Curried Vegetables, 62
Thai Green Curry, 84
Thai Red Curry with Tofu, 102
Thai-Style Pork Kabobs, 144
Three-Topped Rice, 104
Tofu
Buddha's Delight, 94
Chickpea Tikka Masala, 178
Fried Tofu with Asian
Vegetables, 80
Thai Green Curry, 84
Thai Red Curry with Tofu, 102
Tofu Satay Bowl, 108
Tofu Satay Bowl, 108
Tonkatsu (Breaded Pork
Cutlets), 134
Twice-Fried Chicken Thighs with
Plum Sauce, 148

U

Udon Noodles with Chicken and
Spinach, 116

V

Vegetable Lo Mein, 114
Vermicelli with Pork, 86

W

Walnut Chicken, 128
Wasabi Roasted Edamame, 10

Z

Zucchini
Mandarin Orange Chicken, 132
Pakoras, 172
Teppanyaki, 136

METRIC CONVERSION CHART

VOLUME MEASUREMENTS (dry)

$1/8$ teaspoon = 0.5 mL
$1/4$ teaspoon = 1 mL
$1/2$ teaspoon = 2 mL
$3/4$ teaspoon = 4 mL
1 teaspoon = 5 mL
1 tablespoon = 15 mL
2 tablespoons = 30 mL
$1/4$ cup = 60 mL
$1/3$ cup = 75 mL
$1/2$ cup = 125 mL
$2/3$ cup = 150 mL
$3/4$ cup = 175 mL
1 cup = 250 mL
2 cups = 1 pint = 500 mL
3 cups = 750 mL
4 cups = 1 quart = 1 L

VOLUME MEASUREMENTS (fluid)

1 fluid ounce (2 tablespoons) = 30 mL
4 fluid ounces ($1/2$ cup) = 125 mL
8 fluid ounces (1 cup) = 250 mL
12 fluid ounces ($1 1/2$ cups) = 375 mL
16 fluid ounces (2 cups) = 500 mL

WEIGHTS (mass)

$1/2$ ounce = 15 g
1 ounce = 30 g
3 ounces = 90 g
4 ounces = 120 g
8 ounces = 225 g
10 ounces = 285 g
12 ounces = 360 g
16 ounces = 1 pound = 450 g

DIMENSIONS

$1/16$ inch = 2 mm
$1/8$ inch = 3 mm
$1/4$ inch = 6 mm
$1/2$ inch = 1.5 cm
$3/4$ inch = 2 cm
1 inch = 2.5 cm

OVEN TEMPERATURES

250°F = 120°C
275°F = 140°C
300°F = 150°C
325°F = 160°C
350°F = 180°C
375°F = 190°C
400°F = 200°C
425°F = 220°C
450°F = 230°C

BAKING PAN SIZES

Utensil	Size in Inches/Quarts	Metric Volume	Size in Centimeters
Baking or Cake Pan (square or rectangular)	$8 \times 8 \times 2$	2 L	$20 \times 20 \times 5$
	$9 \times 9 \times 2$	2.5 L	$23 \times 23 \times 5$
	$12 \times 8 \times 2$	3 L	$30 \times 20 \times 5$
	$13 \times 9 \times 2$	3.5 L	$33 \times 23 \times 5$
Loaf Pan	$8 \times 4 \times 3$	1.5 L	$20 \times 10 \times 7$
	$9 \times 5 \times 3$	2 L	$23 \times 13 \times 7$
Round Layer Cake Pan	$8 \times 1 1/2$	1.2 L	20×4
	$9 \times 1 1/2$	1.5 L	23×4
Pie Plate	$8 \times 1 1/4$	750 mL	20×3
	$9 \times 1 1/4$	1 L	23×3
Baking Dish or Casserole	1 quart	1 L	—
	$1 1/2$ quart	1.5 L	—
	2 quart	2 L	—